Brad

merry christmas!

Love
Bonnie
Scott

Emily

♥

Jeff

ISLANDS
IN
SPACE
AND
TIME

Books by David G. Campbell

The Ephemeral Islands

The Crystal Desert: Summers in Antarctica

Islands in Space and Time

DAVID G. CAMPBELL

ISLANDS
IN
SPACE
AND
TIME

DESIGNED BY DAVID LARKIN

HOUGHTON MIFFLIN COMPANY
BOSTON   NEW YORK   1996

For information about permission to reproduce selections
from this book, write to Permissions, Houghton Mifflin Company,
215 Park Avenue South, New York, New York 10003.

Campbell, David G.

    Islands in space and time / David G. Campbell.

       p.   cm.

    Includes bibliographical references (p.   ).

    ISBN 0-395-68083-2

    I. Natural areas.   2. Campbell, David G. — Journeys.   I. Title.

  QH75.C25   1996

508 — dc20   96-28388

                                   CIP

Printed in the United States of America

RMT 10 9 8 7 6 5 4 3 2 1

For information about this and other Houghton Mifflin trade and reference books and multi-
media products, visit The Bookstore at Houghton Mifflin on the World Wide Web at
http://www.hmco.com/trade.

Typographic design by Meredith Miller

For George

Contents

Preface

Earth in Middle Age

THE CHAPTERS THAT FOLLOW are accounts of a journey I made across the life-meandered face of this planet to ten places of transcendent natural beauty, where life's bouquet is still redolent and life's signature on the face of the land remains firm, at least for now. I traveled to the montane forests and bogs of Hawaii's Moloka'i, the Andean highlands of Ecuador, Mbaracayú Forest Reserve in Paraguay, Guaraqueçaba and the Baía de Laranjeiras in coastal Brazil, the Maya Mountains of Belize, Río Lagartos in Mexican Yucatán, the Everglades and the Florida Keys, the Flying D Ranch in southwestern Montana, the Río San Pedro in southeastern Arizona, and the Palau Islands in western Micronesia. All of these places are parts of the Nature Conservancy's extensive system of reserves and managed areas and therefore have a good chance of surviving as wilderness.

I made this passage in the summer of my life in an effort to feel a bit more at home on my natal planet. It was also midway through earth's life span, a time when we humans — such a clever and inventive species — are changing everything. We are creating a pulse of extinction as massive as any of those in geological time, including that of the Cretaceous-Tertiary boundary, when the dinosaurs and ammonites went extinct, or the end of the Permian, when the majority of marine genera disappeared. Our presence, etched in extinction, will be discernible for tens of millions of years, and the decisions that we make today regarding the protection of wilderness will alter the course of earthly evolution. Conservationists today are like physicians on the front lines of battle: by necessity they must practice triage.

Using objective criteria, often in circumstances where there are few data, they must choose those areas that are to be conserved and — painfully — those that will be cast aside. No generation of humans has faced a more onerous task.

The Nature Conservancy has had this striking responsibility in mind as it has worked to protect a glittering system of reserves all over the world. Theirs has been one of the great success stories of conservation. Yet the places described in this book are protected by more than fences. They are all components of the Conservancy's new vision, the Last Great Places initiative, which recognizes that in many parts of the world, especially where the human population is burgeoning and poor, the mere acquisition and protection of wild lands are insufficient. Rather than excluding local people, the Conservancy is giving them a clear stake in the success of conservation.

Necessarily, the strategies for conserving and managing the ten places described in this book — and for integrating people into these processes — are as diverse and complex as their biotas and their histories. The chapters of this book, however, are not accounts of the Nature Conservancy's management perspectives. They are instead essays of place, descriptions of lingering wilderness. Each chapter is a time capsule, a snapshot of the moment when we decided to take responsibility for our actions. The sites described here are islands in time and space that have become refuges for some of the varietous invocations of life. Places of hope, they have one thing in common: all have survived triage.

Acknowledgments

The journey described in these essays took me over much of the world during the course of three years. It was the journey of a lifetime, enhanced by the guidance and teaching of persons who have devoted their careers to the conservation of their respective areas. Without them my journey would have been impractical, and this book would have been impossible. I am grateful to Allan C. Randall and Dr. Greg Miller of the Nature Conservancy, Arlington, Virginia; Guy Hughes, formerly of the Nature Conservancy, Maui, Hawaii; Ed Misaki of the Nature Conservancy, Moloka'i; Dr. Xavier Silva del Pozo, former executive director of the Fundación Centro de Datos para la Conservación, Quito, Ecuador; María Helena Jervis, executive director of the Fundación Antisana, Quito; Dr. Kim Hill of the Department of Anthropology, University of New Mexico; Dr. Miguel Morales and Jonathan Padwe of the Fundación Moises Bertoni, Asunción, Paraguay; Ty Kuarangí and Tatunamh'llangi of the Mbaracajú Forest Reserve, Paraguay; Dr. Renato Garcia and Miriam María Garcia of the Universidade Federal do Paraná, Curitiba, Brazil; Dr. Rosita Arvigo, Dr. Gregory Shropshire, and Polo Romero of the Ix Chel Tropical Research Center, San Ignacio, Belize; biologist Luis Gonzales, executive director of PRONATURA, Península de Yucatán, Mérida, Mexico; biologist Joe Keenan of PRONATURA; Eustaquio Massa Trejo of Río Lagartos, Yucatán; Jesús García Barrón, director of the Reserva Río Lagartos; Federico Nava Marin of Mérida; Mark L. Robertson, director of the Florida Keys Initiative, the Nature Conservancy, Key West; Russ Miller, general manager of Turner Enterprises, Inc., Gallatin Gateway, Montana; Bud Griffith of the Flying D Ranch, Gallatin Gateway; Chuck Cook of the Nature Conservancy, Koror, Palau; Captain Bena Sakuma and Margo Vitarelli of Koror; Peg Anderson and Harry Foster, editors at Houghton Mifflin; and Lizzie Grossman of Sterling Lord Literistic. Of course, the opinions expressed in this book are my own and do not necessarily reflect the policies of the Nature Conservancy or the views of the individuals acknowledged above.

Wind-sculpted sand at Río Lagartos.

9

Moloka'i

The Green Heights of Paliuli

Very dark is the ocean and obscure
A sea of coral like the green heights of Paliuli*
The land disappears into them
Covered by the darkness of night
Still it is night.

— Refrain of Chant Two, *The Kumulipo*, a Hawaiian chant of creation

THE HAWAIIANS call the north face of Moloka'i *pali lele koa'e,* "the cliffs where the tropic-birds soar." Legend says that tropicbirds led the first colonists to Hawaii from the Marquesas Islands 1,500 years ago. On clear summer days, you can see the long-tailed white birds vaulting backward in the updrafts, in seeming defiance of the aerodynamics of their wings. These are the highest sea cliffs on earth, reaching to more than 4,000 feet, creating a saw-toothed coast of cloud-shrouded peaks separated by abrupt, green valleys — Waikolu, Pelekunu, Wailau, Papalaua, and Halawa — that plunge to the inaudible sea far below.

Here Moloka'i presents its hunched shoulder to the northeasterly trades — the *mauka* winds — that race unimpeded over the tropical Pacific for thousands of miles, sucking moisture and energy from the warm sea and, once every few millennia, bringing a hopeful colonist. Suddenly bowed by Mount Kamakou, the winds chill, condense into clouds, and drop their moisture. The windward face of Moloka'i is therefore moist and forested, while the southern, leeward side is sunny and arid. This motif of wet and dry is characteristic of the eastern Hawaiian Islands, all of which straddle the wind. For example, on Kaua'i and Oahu, each wet ridge is an island in the sky, and the dry gulf between it and the next ridge, although

---

*Figuratively, Paliuli is a mythical land of the Hawaiian gods where food is ever-abundant. Specifically, the word *paliuli* refers to fertile zones of prolific vegetation in the wet north-facing valleys of Moloka'i, where the heirs of the Hawaiian royal family were raised. Halawa is the *paliuli* where King Kamehameha II spent his childhood.

Cape Halawa, northeastern Moloka'i.

Wailau Valley, northern shore of Moloka'i.

only a few hundred yards wide, is for some species a barrier as daunting as the Sahara. The alternating pockets of wet and dry have provided habitat for a radiation of species — all variations on a few simple themes — unlike any other on earth.

Now and then on the squally lip of Pelekunu Valley, the sheeting fog and rain part, revealing a seeming inversion of land and sky: the sun-bright floor of the valley beneath rain clouds as glowering as the mountains. The vegetation is sheared by the *mauka* trades. Only cringing tussocks of grass, cushion plants, and elfin trees survive here. The fog and rain are nearly constant, and the trees are wrapped in spongy mosses one or two inches thick. The wind-sculpted vegetation becomes waterlogged in the incessant rain, and when the burden becomes too great, the trees snap.

A mile west and nearly a thousand feet beneath the summit of Kamakou, on the slope of Papaala Pali ridge, 4,000 feet above sea level, is a bog, Pepe'opae. Much of the bog is now owned by the Nature Conservancy of Hawaii. It is an earthly treasure, truly a last great place, a lingering vestige of what once was. Only here, and on a few other lonely ridges and mountain tops (some accessible only by helicopter), can one glimpse the nature of Hawaii before humans arrived. These islands, isolated for millions of years and therefore the home of unique and lovely species, have recently become a crossroads for humans and their hitchhikers. The lowlands, especially, have become an alien environment.

You need a good set of boots and four-wheel drive to reach Pepe'opae Bog. Either means of travel takes about the same time. Eighteen inches of rain have fallen this week, and the lower reaches of the road are blocked by fallen eucalyptus trees that must be cleared with a chain saw before we can pass. At 3,000 feet, on the leeward piedmont of the mountain, the forest turns dry and brittle. The ohia lehua trees — a species that has become a symbol of the Hawaiian Islands — predominate here. On this March morning, they are barren of leaves but aflame with red starburst flowers. Their trunks are plaited with lichens the color of copper verdigris. A small flock of *amakihi* (wrenlike honeycreepers) is inspecting the blossoms for nectar. Below, three Pacific golden plovers, annual migrants from the North American tundra, probe the leaf litter. A tawny Hawaiian short-eared owl, mottled yellow and brown like shaggy lichens, dozes silently on a broken stump.

The journey takes all morning, but finally, on the windy ridge of Papaala Pali, one can steep oneself in the true Hawaii. Several species of flowering plants are presenting their sexes to the wind, solitary bees, flies, and the occasional honeycreeper. Many are found only on the isolated mountain tops of the Hawaiian Archipelago: the branching herb *Crytandra procera* (there

The i'iwi, an endemic honeycreeper, is rare today on Moloka'i.

are several other species of *Crytandra* in the Pelekunu Valley below), bushy *Vaccinium*, two species of violets, two species of plantains, red-fruited *Hydrangea*, and shrubs of *Mycine*, with red central leaf veins like swollen arteries. At ground level the recumbent *Lycopodium* club mosses seem to possess a green radiance in the cloud-shrouded light. All the ohia trees are unfolding their blooms. An *apa'pane* honeycreeper, as crimson as the flowers on which it feeds, clings to an ohia tree on the cliff edge, its tail erect; then, tumbling in the cliff wind, it dashes to the next tree.

The *apa'pane* is the most abundant native honeycreeper in the islands, a survivor of repeated invasions of alien birds. The most common bird in the bog today is one of those invaders: the Japanese bush warbler, a short-billed insectivore that clips flies from the blustering wind. Tiny and drab yellow, it is nearly impossible to see in the bonsaied woods, but its voice — eerie and flutelike — is ubiquitous. The Japanese name, *uguisu,* is onomatopoeic, and its song is the reason that the bird was introduced to Oahu in the 1930s. Melodious, perhaps, but destructive. Since its arrival, the *uguisu* has spread to Lana'i, Maui, and Moloka'i, displacing native species. The Japanese bush warbler filled the niche of the native *kakawahie*, a small bird with a short, sharp, almost straight bill also adapted to prying insects from fissures in bark — the island equivalent of a creeper. Last seen in 1963 on the Ohialele Plateau above Pelekunu Valley, the *kakawahie* is almost certainly extinct on Moloka'i. (However, close relatives, all subspecies of the Moloka'i creeper, still survive on Maui, Kaua'i, and the island of Hawaii.)

The Hawaiian Islands are a range of emergent mountain tops, risen from the Central Pacific and isolated in both space and time. The archipelago rambles northwest from the densely populated mountainous islands of Hawaii, Maui, Moloka'i, Lana'i, Oahu, and Kaua'i, to the uninhabited atolls of Laysan, Midway, and Kure. Then at Yuryaku Atoll, 1,050 miles from Hawaii, it veers north. The oldest member of the archipelago, the Emperor Seamount, just south of the Aleutian Trench, is no longer emergent. In its youth, during the last years of the dinosaurs, the seamount may have been as mountainous as Moloka'i; indeed, it was located more or less where that island is today. Its journey — and dissolution — took place an inch at a time.

Each island and atoll in the Hawaiian Archipelago began as a blemish on the sea floor, where the Pacific continental plate, moving northwest at the rate of an inch a year, passed over a weak spot on the earth's crust. There the plastic magma punctured the mantle and escaped as lava, rapidly accumulating into mountains. For seventy million years, the Hawaiian hot spot has remained more or less stationary while the crustal plate has shifted over it. The youngest island, Hawaii (where today Mauna Kea, 13,796 feet high, punctures the snow line, and its angry juvenile neighbor, Kilauea, is actively erupting) is only a few hundred thousand years old — a microsecond in evolutionary time.

Volcanic ash, especially the gassy, vitreous ash of the Hawaiian Archipelago, is soft and friable and readily submits to the rain and to the wind. Once an island drifts off the hot spot and the mountain-building stops, its days are numbered, for the *mauka* rains disassemble the earth itself. The life span of one of these islands, from snowcapped mountain to atoll, is only about 6 million years. Fringed by corals in a warm sea, an island may survive as an atoll for a few million years longer, but eventually it slides north into the cold waters of the temperate Pacific, where its corals succumb. At last only a few smooth pebbles are left to pound and rattle in the shifting surf, and then, in the words of the *Kumulipo*, the dark and obscure ocean returns.

The mountainous islands of the Hawaiian Archipelago have always been isolated in the middle of a wide sea; the nearest continental landmass is more than 1,800 miles away. Although parts of the archipelago have drifted toward Asia, they are eroded to mere nubbins now, and have provided stepping stones for only the most salt-tolerant colonists. All of

Hawaii's ancestral plants and animals were necessarily vagabonds, drifters on currents of ocean or air or hitchhikers on birds. Successful colonizations were extremely rare. The entire native flora of the Hawaiian Islands, which before the arrival of people totaled about 1,200–1,300 species (of which 90 percent were endemic), evolved from only 300 successful introductions, the equivalent of approximately one every 250,000 years. The greatest number (40 percent) of the plant colonists came from the Indo-Pacific (and ultimately, therefore, tropical Asia); about 20 percent came from the Americas. Some 75 percent of these plants were hitchhikers on birds, either externally or internally; the rest were waifs adapted to drifting on the wind and

A flowering ohia lehua tree growing on a lava flow.

the sea. Ferns and mosses, whose spores are not much bigger than a cell, were among the first to take hold. By providing a low canopy and shade from the burning sun and by creating organic soil, they set the stage for subsequent colonizers.

The successful landfall of a spore stuck to the feather of a bird is easy to imagine, but survival in the new environment was the real challenge. Most colonists rapidly died out. Even today the islands are conspicuously lacking entire orders and families of plants and animals that are common on the nearest continents. The island biotas are disharmonic, in the parlance of ecologists. For example, only 15 percent of the families of arthropods that one would expect to find in comparable latitudes in Asia or North America have successfully colonized here. There are no chiggers or ticks. In this archipelago of hungry birds, there are only two species of colorful day-flying native butterflies (yet about 950 species of secretive night-flying moths). Like the plants, the entire native Hawaiian insect fauna, an estimated 10,000 species, is descended from only 350 to 400 successful landfalls.

The colonists that made it diversified into a medley of unfilled niches that did not exist on the crowded continental mainland. Their speciation was accelerated by the inconstancy of the volcanic islands. Lava flows, especially the ropy — *pahoehoe* — lava, are fickle, their course easily diverted by a slight undulation in terrain, a boulder, or a cooling along one edge. These meanders often surrounded refuges of vegetation, islands within islands known as *kipukas*, that were spared immolation. Although most *kipukas* persisted for only a few centuries, this was sufficient time for thousands of generations of insects and other short-lived organisms. Over millennia the repeated dissection of habitats — through the dramatic orogeny of mountains and valleys, the formation of *kipukas*, the dichotomy of wet and dry — isolated small populations. This isolation fostered the genesis of new species through the process known as adaptive radiation, which is characteristic of archipelagos. For example, on Oahu, the wet- and dry-sided valleys of the Koolau Range have led to the radiative evolution of over thirty species of *Cyanea*, in the lobelia family. The fifty-four species of Hawaiian honeycreepers are all descended from a single ancestor that arrived from tropical America. Among the Hawaiian insects as many as one hundred species are typically descended from a single colonizing ancestor.

The most extravagant insect radiations have been among the moths in the genus *Hyposmocoma*, which has about 550 species, and the Hawaiian fruit flies, about 820 species in two genera, *Drosophila* and *Scaptomyza*. The astonishing radiation in fruit flies is not entirely explainable by geographical isolation alone. Male Hawaiian fruit flies engage in elaborate

A Drosophila fruit fly.

courtship rituals known as lekking, in which they conspicuously display the designs in their wings from an exposed leaf. Slight differences in behavior or in visual display — mediated by change in a single gene — can reproductively isolate entire populations from their antecedent neighbors.

As the old islands wore down and new ones emerged to the southeast, the immigrant life forms had to jump ship or perish. The middle-aged islands — Kaua'i, Oahu, and Moloka'i — are the most diverse, since they have had sufficient time to acquire and differentiate their species and have not yet lost them. Kaua'i was the source of many of the ancestors of the species that have so extravagantly radiated to the newer and more mountainous islands to the east. But Kaua'i is eroding rapidly; Waimea Canyon, sometimes called the Grand Canyon of the Pacific, will divide the island in two in another million years or so.

The first successful colonizers were necessarily preadapted to the salty shores and arid conditions of the leeward lowlands. It was left to their descendants to colonize the moist highlands. This contingency is etched in the biological diversity of the islands today: the dry coastal forests harbor more species of woody plants than the moist upland tropical forests, and most of the tropical forest species have a xeric ancestor. There is a strange benignity to these forests, both wet and dry. During their long residency in a disharmonic environment without natural enemies, many plant species lost their defenses, which were expensive in terms of energy and nutrients to produce and largely unnecessary on an island with no large herbivores. Blackberries lost their spines; mints their piquancy.

Disharmony has enabled radiations into unoccupied niches. Yellow-flowered thistles grow to the size of trees. The green-winged inchworm larvae of moths in the genus *Epithecia* stalk and hunt fruit flies — the only predatory caterpillars on earth. On islands where the trade winds can blow an animal to its death out at sea, wings have become a liability; flightlessness is a common adaptation among the lacewings, moths, beetles, crickets, katydids, leafhoppers, and wasps. Hawaiian geese are flightless also. Other organisms have developed exquisite mutualisms. High in the mountains, where the *mauka* winds drop their moisture, the honeycreepers and the lobelioids evolved together in a race for the sky; the floral corollas of the lobelioids exactly match the anatomy of their pollinators' beaks.

A predatory inchworm.

The most successful were necessarily generalists, able to fit into a variety of habitats and to hold on. The ohia tree, probably a relatively recent arrival, is a good example. It grows on both dry and wet mountain flanks and produces flowers, in a taxonomy-defying range of sizes and morphologies, most months of the year. It is the dominant tree on the new volcanic lands of the Big Island. Most ancestors of highland tropical forest species began this way. Specialization — and, later, speciation — came only after the long isolation of small populations in the various microhabitats of the islands.

Moloka'i, thirty-eight miles long and 2 million years old, is relatively small and youthful. It is part of a huge oceanic shelf known as Maui Nui, that also includes the islands of Lana'i, Maui, and Kahoolawe. Punctured by six volcanoes, Maui Nui is now mostly submerged, but at least four times during the Pleistocene Epoch, when icecaps smothered much of the Northern Hemisphere and sea levels dropped as much as 300 feet worldwide, the sandy banks of the shelf were exposed, creating vast, windy, largely arid lowlands between the volcanic peaks. The four islands were one large landmass then and had many common species. But after the glaciers melted, the intruding sea separated the volcanoes once more; in isolation, new species evolved. Today, the islands of Maui Nui share many vicariant species, which, like the honeycreepers, are all variations on a theme.

Every winter Alaskan humpback whales migrate to Maui Nui to give birth to and nurse their calves in the tranquil seas between the islands. The mothers stay on the western side of Maui, in the lee of the huge volcanoes of Haleakala and Puu Kukui. But the males and frisky juveniles relish the tumult of the channel between Moloka'i and Maui, especially the wind-edge where the placid leeward water abruptly erupts in spray, making their blows indistinguishable from the whitecaps and sea spatter. For most of their trip to and from Alaska and their residency in Hawaii, the humpbacks fast. The clear, warm Hawaiian waters do not have enough food to make it worthwhile for the whales to conduct their laborious filter-feeding, pushing their baleen-plated mouths through the sea. But on the southern shore of Moloka'i, where the rich volcanic land bleeds into the sea, there are blooms of phytoplankton and therefore an abundance of fish. That is why, in the thirteenth century, the Hawaiians built fish corrals out of the ragged native rock of this productive coast. When the pilchards are running, a few male humpbacks visit these shores to snack on the wine of the land. The boldest come into the shallows on the far side of the lagoon, just beyond the breaking reef, and on still nights you can hear them slap the water with their flukes.

Along the southern shore of Moloka'i, the various strata of volcanic ash look like a multilayered cake. Today these dry lowlands are almost devoid of native vegetation, instead bearing the scars of worn-out pineapple plantations and ranches. The land is as visually boring as a midwestern soybean field: tumbling tussocks of sweet vernal grass, velvet grass, and kikuyu grass, all aggressive African or Eurasian invaders that have replaced the native bunch grass that once grew interspersed with the dry forests.

Only a sparse fossil record hints of the strange biota that the Marquesans encountered upon their arrival in the islands. Conditions must have been near Edenic. Fossil sites dating from the Ice Ages have yielded at least fifty species of flightless birds, most of which were denizens of the lowland forests and all of which are extinct today. In the Moʻomomi dunes, eroded by the *mauka* winds in a coastal swale west of Mount Kamakou, dense beds of fossil root casts, blackened by the sun, emerge from a strand that today is besieged by alien grasses and forbs. The casts hint of the tree species that once prospered in the lowlands. The dunes cover the remains of about thirty bird species, ten of which are now extinct, including a sea eagle, a flightless goose, a falconing owl, a giant crow, and a stubby-legged flightless ibis that probed the coastal forest understory with its blunt, curved bill, much like a kiwi. The native Hawaiians used to spend their summers in these dunes, catching and drying fish. Their basalt tools still litter the area. It seems likely that they hunted these species to extinction, for at other sites, the bones of extinct birds are found near their caves and cooking hearths.

The decline of the Hawaiian biota, therefore, began long before the European arrival. The native Hawaiians brought twenty-seven, perhaps as many as thirty-three, species of plants with them. They introduced the carbohydrate-rich staples of taro and sugar cane, but also the dog, the jungle fowl, the dwarf Polynesian pig, the Pacific rat and, inadvertently, the adventive land snail. Just as important, the Marquesans brought fire.

The first settlement on Molokaʻi, about A.D. 650, was in the Halawa Valley on the eastern end of the island. Eventually settlers spread west to the adjacent Wailau and Pelekunu valleys. These valleys, which are the inspirations for the Paliuli myth, were carved from the steep mountains of the north coast, between the black beaches and waterfall-bannered ramparts. Their rivers leak sediments into the sea, creating turbid bays. The Hawaiians built their houses on the low flanks of the valleys beyond the reach of tsunamis. They transformed the valley floors into plantations of sweet potato and taro, and when the weather permitted, fished offshore from canoes. Populations were small: in 1836, Pelekunu had 218 people; by 1900 it supported only 32.

The valleys have very different personalities. Halawa, the widest, is crossed by a meandering river, and its flanks are arid from the desiccating hot winds rising from the valley floor. Wailau is steep-walled and broad. Pelekunu, which means "stinking valley" in Hawaiian

The mouth of the Halawa Valley.

(a reference to its ever-wet climate and the concomitant stench of decomposition), is narrow and sun-starved. Harriet Ne, who lived in Pelekunu from 1915 to 1921, wrote, "Pelekunu's people, in the days I remember, would rise early — perhaps at five-thirty every morning — to make use of the sun for their chores." By early afternoon the sun would set, and the valley would be wrapped in a damp penumbra.

By the time James Cook landed at Waimea Bay, Kaua'i, on January 18, 1778, the Hawaiian Islands had been inhabited for nearly a millennium. The islands had already been diminished of their full complement of species by the activities of the Polynesians. At least two-thirds of the native birds, including all of the flightless species and at least fifteen species of honeycreepers, were extinct. Ten percent of the native plants, particularly those species that lived only in the dry, lowland forests, were gone. Cook observed a land already transformed by humans: plantations of taro, plantain, sugar cane, sweet potatoes "as big as a mans head," and the Chinese paper mulberry tree. On the beach there was "a brisk trade for pigs, fowls and roots which was carried on with the greatest good order." The lowland forests had been decimated. "Although we saw very few trees except the Cocoanut tree, they must have some of a good size on which they make their canoes; as they are in general about twenty four feet long and . . . for the most part formed of one piece." At the time of Cook's arrival there may have been 300,000 to 500,000 native Hawaiians, but within a few decades Western diseases had reduced their numbers to less than 15,000. Even Cook anticipated the destructive potential of introduced pestilence. "As there were some venereal complaints on board both the Ships, in order to prevent its being communicated to these people, I gave orders that no Women, on any account whatever were to be admitted on board the Ships."

Moloka'i was spared European contact until the early 1800s, when King Kamehameha II ordered the men of the island to cut the fragrant sandalwood, which grew only at the middle elevations of the windward mountain faces and was sold to the Chinese for carvings. The trade in sandalwood started the decline of the moist forests. The king ordered his people to dig pits exactly the size of the cargo ships; when the pits were filled with logs the chiefs would negotiate with foreign captains, usually Europeans, for the entire shipload. Eventually the Hawaiian workers rebelled against the exploitation; they pulled up sandalwood seedlings and ring-barked the adult trees to deprive their chiefs of the lucrative resource. The pits remain today, but sandalwood is nearly extinct.

*

Half of Hawaii's rain forest and 90 percent of its lowland dry forest have now been destroyed. Five plant species are represented by single individuals, and twelve are reduced to such vestigial numbers that their extinction is imminent. The most pernicious threat today is not direct destruction of habitat but the indirect effects of newly arrived species. Before the arrival of humans in the islands, a new plant colonization occurred once every 250,000 years or so. Now the botanical invasion rate is nearly nine million times greater. Thirty-five aliens, of which twelve to fifteen are new insect pests, arrive every year; jetliners and first-class mail are the principal vectors. The islands are being overwhelmed. In the 1880s, about 150 alien plant species were recorded; today there are 861, including those introduced by the Polynesians before 1778. Many are aggressive species, adapted to highly competitive, harmonic mainland communities. They easily overwhelm the mild-mannered natives, which lack spines and poisons. The prickly thimbleberry and spiny blackberry both displace the unarmed native Hawaiian raspberry. Some invaders, such as the banana poka (a passionflower vine from South America), were introduced as ornamentals. The banana poka has showy flowers and bounteous fruits, which are enthusiastically dispersed by birds. Today the banana poka has choked over 70,000 acres, particularly in the upland, forested areas of Hawaii and Kaua'i. (Ironically, the caterpillars of two exotic moths, *Cyanotricha necyria* and *Pyrausta perelegans,* are being tested as control agents for the plant.) On all the large islands, the tropical American strawberry guava, whose delicious fruits are dispersed by feral hogs, creates dense, tangled monocultures. Fifteen species of Melastomaceae, a family of shrubs of tropical America and Asia, which were cultivated because of their attractive hairy, lyre-veined leaves, have become rampant weeds.

Exotic diseases, which so ravaged the native Hawaiians, have been equally devastating to wildlife. Avian malaria, vectored by introduced mosquitoes, is wiping out the remaining lowland birds. At present, no mosquitoes survive above 5,000 feet, which may explain why many of the remaining native birds are found only above that altitude.

Larger animals, of course, can be weeds, too. Alien fruit flies — the Mediterranean, oriental, and melon — have displaced a number of native fruit flies and become agricultural pests. The tropical American marine toad, rats, domestic cats, and the small Indian mongoose have devoured most of the remaining ground-dwelling birds. Ungulates are the most conspicuous invaders. In 1867, seven axis deer, three bucks and four does, were introduced to Moloka'i, gifts from the Hawaiian consul in Hong Kong to King Kamehameha V. A Dr. William Hillebrand was specially dispatched to Calcutta to capture and transport the deer to the islands. Their arrival in Honolulu was described in the *Pacific Commercial Advertiser* on December 21, 1867:

> These really beautiful animals, the spotted Indian deer brought by the *Lock Na Garr*, which lies at the market wharf, have been visited by many of our residents the past week. On Wednesday one of the hinds gave birth to a fine kid, as healthy and frisky as if born in his own mountain home. It is a male, and the officers of the ship have named him Kamehameha VI. As the ship goes to sea tomorrow, the deer will be transferred to the King's yacht, and taken to Moloka'i, where we hope they will rapidly increase and stock the whole island.

Axis deer, beautiful but destructive.

The deer prospered beyond the wildest hopes of the naive reporter. At first they invaded the southern lowlands and dry mountain valleys of the eastern half of the island. By 1898 the deer had defoliated much of eastern Moloka'i. They had become a cloven-hoofed plague, removing the low browse and opening the understory. Two full-time hunters from the American mainland were brought to the island and paid forty dollars a month plus whatever they could earn by selling the skins. Local hunters were also hired. One, R. W. Meyer, was reputed to be able to lift two bucks, one under each arm, and carry them out of the steep-sided mountain valleys. In the first two years the hired hunters killed about 10,000 deer, but it wasn't enough. The deer fled to the low volcanic nubbin of western Moloka'i, where they were given some protection by the privately owned Moloka'i Ranch, and they proliferated anew.

Feral pigs have been a greater problem for a longer time. In an archipelago with only two species of native mammals (the hoary bat and the monk seal) the first pigs, like the Marquesans who brought them there, must have found the islands Edenic. The dwarf Polynesian pigs, known as *pua'a,* had the trim economy suited to travel by canoe over the open sea, and they consumed less food than their Asian ancestors. At first, *pua'a* meat was so scarce that only royal males were allowed to eat it, but soon the pigs escaped into the lowland forest and proliferated boundlessly. History has not recorded the effect of the Polynesian pigs on the native vegetation and on the ground-nesting birds and invertebrates, but it must have been catastrophic. The islands were transmuted as much by hogs as by direct human activities. A thousand years later, larger, more aggressive Eurasian hogs came to the islands. They readily bred with the *pua'a,* and the newly vigorous hybrids spread over the islands like animate fire.

Hogs continue to be important in the culture of native Hawaiians. They are especially prized on Moloka'i, which is a traditional retreat of kings and which today is experiencing a renaissance of native Hawaiian culture. Legend states that the Hawaiian royalty are all descended from a union between Pele, the god of volcanism, and Kamapua'a, a human-pig Chimera. Yet hogs commit terracide. Their voracity is a direct function of their intelligence. They eat native vegetation, crush the seeds of native fruits without dispersing them, nuzzle out buried roots and tubers, create wallows that become the breeding ground for the alien *Culex* mosquitoes that carry avian malaria. In recent years their population has soared because of the surfeit of food afforded by other aliens, particularly banana poka and guava.

In 1989 the Nature Conservancy began a program of pig control at Kamakou and Pelekunu, confining them with fences, trapping them with snares, and encouraging people to hunt them. Although rational and necessary, the program offended many sectors of Hawaiian society. The native Hawaiians argued that hogs were as necessary to their culture as taro or sugar cane. Even traditional enemies, such as the Hawaiian Humane Society and hunters' organizations, united against the Conservancy. The snares, they argued, were left unattended for days at a time, subjecting the pigs to a lingering, painful death and wasting the meat. The snares also caught dogs. A solution to the problem has been elusive, for it involves a complex interplay of the rights of humans to maintain their traditional culture, of animals to be treated humanely and, ultimately, of the land to keep its integrity.

The rain-buffeted Kamakou Plateau, the Pepe'opae bog, and the plunging Pelekunu Valley are among the last vestiges of the Hawaiian alpine wilderness. Cold, wet, or steep, these places are largely inhospitable to humans, mosquitoes, and most of the other Johnny-come-latelies that are displacing the native wildlife. They are a refuge — for now. Too much has already been lost; most of the rest is doomed. The spoor of hogs is everywhere: nuzzled roots, muddy wallows and trails. Ultimately, the pigs must be banished if this land is to survive, if there is to be any trace of what the Marquesans encountered here 1,500 years ago.

Cayambe Coca

The Plain of Sky

THE CATHEDRAL OF SAN FRANCISCO, in the Old Town of Quito, Ecuador, is built of the granites and young, angry basalts of the volcanoes that surround the city. Recently the cathedral was almost knocked down by earthquakes, and its arches and walls are reinforced by crude wood. San Francisco is a good place to contemplate the beginnings of the New World. It is a symbol of conquest, both political and ecological. Sitting on a coarse wooden pew next to a red and white altar to Santa Claus, I watch a little girl carry a candle down the aisle, her face lambent. Above her is the dark vault, redolent with the terpenic incense of palo santo wood, its far reaches abounding with demons and saints, murals of heaven and hell. The blue dome is painted with big, yellow, childish stars. The pulpit is supported by wooden statues of straining Indian peasants. They are not happy.

Outside, the broad cathedral square is silent except for the mournful cry of a dove. Quito, nearly two miles above sea level, is surrounded by mountain ramparts. Like the cathedral, the city is a place of shadow and light. The air is washed with clouds that slink down the slopes and fill the valley with an undulating mist that clarifies several times a day. On the steeper slopes, the vapors tumble, giving the dreamy appearance of slow waterfalls.

Gonzalo Pizarro, brother of Francisco, the *conquistador* who subdued the Incas, became governor of Quito in 1539, only six years after the collapse of the Inca empire and forty-seven years after the Spanish arrival in the New World. In 1534 the Franciscans, the order of brown-hooded monks who followed the pestilence and bloodshed of conquest, started construction of the cathedral, the first Spanish church in South America. In the cathedral square, the Franciscans sowed a field of wheat, the first of its kind in the Americas,

29

and brought their domesticated Eurasian animals — sheep, goats, cattle, and hogs — which would transform the landscape of Ecuador as much as any army could. The local Quitus, Quichuas, and Otavalos had few domestic animals: semiwild llamas and alpacas, dogs and guinea pigs. However, the diversity of their domesticated plants was unrivaled on earth: amaranth, arborescent tomatoes, corn, potatoes, and other tubers. They had as many names for varieties of potatoes — each with a particular size, flavor, and texture — as Eskimos had for snow. This was the true gold of the Spanish conquest; these were the species that transformed the diet, and therefore the history, of the world.

For the Quitus, the Spanish were the last of several conquerors. During the ninth and tenth centuries, the Caras Indians, from the fertile mountain valleys to the south, subdued the agricultural Quitus. They brought art, math, and science, and readily intermarried with their victims. At the end of the fifteenth century, the Incas, inspired by the charismatic Huayna Capac, began invading central Ecuador. It was a prolonged and desultory battle. North of Quito, at Yaguarcocha Lake (Blood Lake), a fierce struggle was waged until the water was suffused with the blood of warriors. The invasion was stopped at the Cochasqui pyramids, where 10,000 Quitus-Caras were besieged for over a year. The resistance there is the reason that the Incas never conquered southern Colombia and that the Otavalo Indians, who live between Quito and the Colombian border, retain their own distinct culture, language, and clothing.

The Inca invasion was interrupted in 1520, when runners brought news of the Spanish arrival on the isthmus of Panamá. In their bodies the messengers brought an Old World disease — probably smallpox — that was the true *conquistador.* History does not record how many thousands the pestilence killed in the highlands around Quito, except that Huayna Capac succumbed, and with him the will of his people. When Huayna Capac died, according to Cieza de León, "The lamentation and shrieks rose to the skies, causing the birds to fall to the ground" (cited in Crosby, p. 55).

The Incas' lamentations were more than metaphorical. The ecological conquest of Latin America came about through the introduction of new and aggressive species of plants and animals, the imposition of cattle and sheep ranching, and the establishment of an economic system that consumed forests. It brought the greatest changes in the continent since the closure of the Darién Gap, 2.4 million years earlier, when North American placental mammals overwhelmed the insular South American marsupials. With the arrival of the Spanish, all the rules of survival changed in the New World.

*

The permanently frozen crown of Cayambe volcano.

On a clear day, looking west from the promontory of Cochasqui, one can see the entire snow-capped panorama of what the polymath explorer Alexander von Humboldt named "the Avenue of the Volcanoes." It is the Andean spine of northern Ecuador: Cayambe, Sarahurco, Pambamarca, Gualimburo, Cerro Puntas (which has the unreal appearance of a series of sine waves), Antisana, Sincholagua, Cotopaxi, and Rumiñahui. The Incas personified each peak and endowed it with a mythology; each was afflicted with envy, jealousy, and love.

These cordilleras and valleys create strings of archipelagos as much as any sea does. Not all of the mountains are volcanic. Some are plated in calcium carbonate rock, embedded with fossils of mollusks and ammonites folded from marine sediments. Each range, and its valleys, is isolated. The windward sides of the mountains are rain-lashed by clouds that rise from either the Amazon or the Pacific lowlands; their lee sides are dry. On the ridges you can walk from drizzle to sun in a few seconds.

But the deep valleys, called *abrigadas,* in the rain shadows of the tallest mountains, are semiarid. The *abrigadas* create their own microclimates, and even in the height of the rainy season, from the end of September to early April, they remain dry and dusty. The vegetation is dry-deciduous. On this January afternoon the high valley around Quito is pelted with cold rain, but the nearby *abrigadas* are sunny. Century plants and bromeliads cling to the brows of the hillsides denuded by sheep and goats. The soil is sloughing into the Guayllabamba River valley below. Sometimes a whole facet of a mountain falls into the river, which is small and narrow. The canyon becomes temporarily dammed, and a vast volume of water builds up. A few days later, the dam bursts, inundating the valley floor as well as settlements and farms downstream.

Only the sky, which shifts from sullen to transparent in a few minutes, is untamed here. These isolated Andean valleys have been cultivated for millennia. The array of Andean domesticated plants started here. The genes of the crop species were shuffled and recombined by repeated human invasions and by sinuous lines of taxation and tribute. However, when the Spanish brought sugar cane, a cash crop from the Old World, and cultivated it in the *abrigadas,* the native crops were displaced. Today, except for a few straggling acacias, little of the original vegetation is left.

As in Moloka'i, most of life's diversity is diminished by the journey to high altitude. In the *ceja de la montaña* (eyebrow of the mountain), the green forested ridges and deep river valleys of the Andean escarpment, the varied bouquet of lowland species is distilled into a few fragrances. And quickly, too. Higher still, the sky islands appear, each with startling and strange endemic species, relics that cling in isolation to the pates of the cloud-shrouded peaks. The composites — resourceful flowering plants that have evolved relatively recently — are especially prosperous here. Daisies that are herbaceous in the lowland zones become woody and arborescent in the highlands. To see the tree daisies, I journey north from Quito with Professor Xavier Silva del Pozo, an entomologist who is director of Ecuador's Conservation Data Center. Xavier's job, which is coordinated with the Nature Conservancy, is to take stock of Ecuadorian species and habitats that are unique and endangered in order to set priorities for conservation. Like a physician treating wounded soldiers on the front line, Xavier practices triage. It's as much an art as a science. He must assign value to the intangible, to aesthetics. He must quantify the unknown, guessing how many species exist in an area where the total number of species is uncounted — indeed, where many species have never been described and never will be, given the rates of habitat destruction. There are no right choices, just considered guesses.

Xavier and I take a cobbled Inca trail over the sheep-gnawed fields into the clouds in the northern province of Carchi. The trail was one of the sinews of the Inca empire; it was down this same road that the runners brought the news and the pathogens of the Spanish invasion in 1520. Today the Inca trails are wide enough for a Jeep, but in the drenching rain, the road is a river. We are headed to the Páramo del Angel (Plain of the Angel), the last refuge of the *frailejónes*, the giant tree daisies (*fraile* means "monk," a reference to the daisies' nodding habit). The locals call this type of vegetation a *páramo de lluvia*, or rain paramo. In these waterlogged moors, where temperatures drop to near freezing at night, plant litter decomposes slowly and thick beds of peat accumulate; in some places the land is so spongy that it quakes and undulates under one's feet. When the clouds part and the wind pauses, it is suddenly — briefly — burning hot. The ancient roadside has the characteristic plants of the paramo: low shrubs attired in lichens and orchids. The land is cloaked in bright yellow foliating mosses, red-flowering fuchsias, bright green trailing *Selaginella* — a primitive relative of the mosses — and a few resolute ferns. Drooping purple daisies hang their faces toward the earth, seeking protection from the rain and burning sunlight. They are battered by hungry flies seeking shelter, a valuable resource here and an inducement to pollinators. Many species are recumbent, slinking in the wind-shadows of rocks, presenting the least possible area to the bright, drying sky.

33

Tree daisies on the Páramo del Ángel

The *frailejónes* grow above the Pacific *ceja*, starting at 10,800 feet, in a wide cirque around a chalky turquoise lake that drops a rivulet into the clouds. The millions of *frailejónes* on the Plain of the Angel look like a crowd of pilgrims in a square. Each presents a rosette of slender gray-green leaves and yellow inflorescences, like bundles of shaggy sunflowers, to the changing sky. There are three generations of leaves on each tree. The new leaves are downy, covered with translucent hairs, a protection against the unfiltered sunlight at high altitude. The older leaves, tucked safely under the shading rosette, are bald. The dead leaves accumulate under the rosettes like the brown robes of a monk; long after the rain ends they drip disconsolately. In the *sol de água* (water-sun), the ground breathes white vapor into the still, clear air. Sound and light travel deceptively far here. The silence is slashed by the raspy call of a hawk turning over the cirque, and the air fills with the nearly inaudible thrum of countless clear-winged flies, which, along with moths, supplant bees as pollinators at high altitudes. An eared owl, exactly the color of the new leaves of the *frailejón* on which it perches, waits for night.

A spectacled bear.

The Páramo del Angel, where Ecuador's last remaining spectacled bears, tapirs, and pumas live, was recently declared a protected area. It is a remote and inhospitable region with little traditional economic value, but now demographic pressures are forcing people into such marginal zones, and the paramo is being used for pasture. Shepherds regularly burn the coarse, mature grasses to promote the tender young shoots that are the delight of the sheep. Some of the *frailejónes* bear the scars of fire, and the soil beneath them is charred. Now, a few months after the burn, the sprouting new grasses refract the sunlight like filiform lenses. Each tussock displays all textures and shades of green, twirled by the wind and the rain. These fires may have led to the extinction of several species, including the blood-red paramo toad, which was last recorded in 1988. But the leaf litter is alive with invertebrates. I tip over a volcanic bomb and find scorpions, along with red-and-white walking sticks, which hold their tails curled and erect, mimicking their neighbors. Mimicry is cheap protection: there are far more walking sticks than scorpions.

The village of Santa Bárbara, almost exactly on the Colombian border, is perched on the Amazonian *ceja* forty-five miles east of the Páramo del Angel, at an altitude of 8,450 feet. The streets around the central square and church are cobbled. The red-tiled houses have no chimneys; the smoke from the domestic fires seeps through the roof shingles, nourishing abundant mosses and even a few ferns. Laundry hangs above a roof like a string of prayer flags. Today the square is deserted; everybody is gathering potatoes in the mountains above.

Tree daisies on the escarpment of the Páramo del Angel.

Most of the forest of the Amazonian *ceja* has been converted into farms and looks moth-eaten. This is a quilted landscape, stitched with windrows of trees. Here in the *campo* the way of life — the crops, the wooden plows, the communal management of the land — has changed little since pre-Columbian times. Only coffee, bananas, the oxen that pull the plows, and the sheep that shave the paramo are post-conquest. The *campesinos* traditionally grow their crops in newly burned soil, which has fewer diseases and insect pests and is temporarily fertilized by the ash. They are planted in duplets. Plantains provide the shading canopy demanded by coffee bushes. In the Amazonian lowlands, manioc, a traditional root crop that is almost pure starch, is planted under an overstory of corn. After a decade of continuous use, the soil has so many fungal diseases, nematodes, and other pests that further harvests require the liberal application

of pesticides. When the expenditure for chemicals becomes prohibitive, the land is abandoned and new areas are cleared. But new land is running out, and secondary forest is being cut down before it can recover its species richness.

On the tilted plain around Santa Bárbara, the farmers' plots seem nearly vertical and almost inaccessible. Sheep trails corrugate the slopes. During the dry summer, hot winds roam the hillsides and remove the soil from the bald patches. When the clouds part, light plays over the denuded hills, revealing every fold and edge. January is potato-harvesting season, and white gunnysacks slouch in the fields like exhausted peasants. Entire families, even toddlers, are digging and heaping the bounty. Some have set up tents in the fields in order to grab a nap. Dressed in rain-soaked woolens, they toil, indifferent to deluge and burning sun.

The ceja de la montaña *on the Amazonian escarpment of the Andes.*

Beneath the *ceja*, the lowland forest canopy closes in, and except for occasional treefalls and river courses, continues fast and shady all the way to the Atlantic, 2,500 miles east. More vegetation zones are crammed into this descending slope, each with its own particular suite of species, than almost anywhere else on earth. All are bathed in the rising Amazonian vapors, which on the lower reaches condense into torrential rain showers and on the cloud-forested highlands hang as shrouds of mist and fog. The forests of the *ceja* are biologically unexplored. Only the conspicuous birds and mammals have been adequately recorded. Perhaps as much as 20 percent of the species of flowering plants have yet to be described (the actual number is, by definition, unknowable), and the majority of insect species are uncatalogued.

The Cayambe-Coca Ecological Reserve, 996,070 acres straddling four provinces and ten life zones, from the Andean cordillera across the *ceja* into the Amazon Valley, was established in 1970. The reserve also embraced the ranges of three isolated indigenous tribes, whose combined population was only four hundred: the Quichua-Oyacachi, Quichua-Quijo, and Cofán. With the establishment of the reserve, the Indians were given title to their lands for the first time since the Spanish conquest.

But new economic forces changed everything. In 1968 oil was discovered in the northeastern sector of Napo Province. At a time when global oil prices were soaring, Ecuador had a surfeit of cheap fuel. Petroleum became a cornerstone for the central planners of this mountainous country. Soon a pipeline and its service road vaulted the Andean cordillera. In 1987 the pipeline ruptured, spilling 65,000 barrels of crude oil into the Amazon Valley, and during repairs another 15,000 barrels leaked into the Río Quijos. But it was the road, more than the pipeline, that brought the most calamitous changes. The local tribes were overwhelmed by the arrival of 51,500 *campesinos*, mostly hopeful refugees from the urban squalor of Quito or the feudal repression of nearby *hidalgos*. Land-hungry peasants, evangelists, and other hopeful adventurers migrated down the road and settled along its margins. It was a politically volatile situation. Most of the *colonos* were squatters, denied legal access to the new lands. They led a marginal existence on soils that were rapidly becoming senile and unusable for crops. To supplement their incomes, the *colonos* poached trees from the reserve — easy pickings with little risk. A ready market for wood products existed among the artisans of the nearby villages, and a single log of *copal* (*Protium*) or *cedro* (cedar) was worth several years' wages. Sawed by hand in the forest, a tree could be smuggled out of the reserve in the form of boards.

The Cofán, who today number only eighty-four and therefore have negligible political clout, were the most affected by the opening of the interior. The petroleum extraction fragmented their tribal lands, and their new titles suddenly became useless. However, as during the Spanish conquest four hundred years before, it was pathogens, especially Western respiratory infections and "childhood" diseases, more than direct appropriation of their land, that precipitated their decline. Both the Cofán and the forest around them are vestiges of what they once were. In a dying land, the youths who have survived infancy flee to the cities and are assimilated by Western culture.

A quilted tapestry of farms near Otavalo, Ecuador.

The Nature Conservancy helped draft a management plan for the violated reserve, but there were no easy answers. Restrictions were placed on the extraction of wood and on gold mining, the conventional means of earning a quick and substantial income from the forest and its rivers. As alternatives, the management plan called for reforestation projects, fish farming, and agricultural cooperatives. But these are long-term strategies, and squatters, accustomed to living from day to day, are impatient for riches. When their livelihoods became illegal, many moved on, becoming refugees once more.

Since the establishment of the Cayambe-Coca Ecological Reserve, the population of Ecuador has more than doubled, and the demands on the environment have increased rather than diminished. At current rates of logging and slash-and-burn farming, Ecuador will be entirely deforested by 2025. The *ceja* and its panoply of species are for the most part doomed. Most of the battle is to stave off environmental bankruptcy so that people can make a sustained living from the fragile and diminished land. Conservation of biological diversity is a secondary goal. The places that will survive as wilderness, if any, are now being chosen by Xavier Silva del Pozo and his colleagues. Their painful triage is the last act of the conquest.

Certain glamorous species have become national icons, rallying points for conservation. In China it is the panda. In Ecuador it is the Andean condor, which with a wingspan of nine feet is the largest land bird in the Americas. Enormous attention is being devoted to these survivors. Some have argued that resources are being squandered on what are basically relics, highly specialized animals that were doomed anyway, and that the money would be better spent on preserving entire species-rich habitats, such as the *ceja de la montaña*. Others would say that pandas and condors are like miners' canaries, symptomatic of overall environmental health; saving them would save the entire ecosystem.

Once ubiquitous through the Ecuadorian highlands, today the condors number less than one hundred. Twenty-three, the largest population in the country, live in the region of Antisana, a dormant volcano just south of Cayambe-Coca. The first European to describe Antisana was Humboldt, who in 1802 spent three weeks in a stone house at the base of the mountain. Humboldt, acknowledged as the founder of several disciplines, including biogeography, was quintessentially curious and was beloved everywhere he traveled. When news of his death in 1859 reached Quito, the bells of San Francisco tolled dolefully. What did this ascete perceive in this mountain fastness? We know that he wrote of the orogeny of the Avenue of the Volcanoes, which thrilled and confused him.

An Andean condor.

He wondered how fossil ammonites, discovered at an elevation of over 12,000 feet just south of here on the slopes of Chimborazo, could have made their way to these snowy peaks. He pondered the transience of the mountains.

I spent a day with María Helena Jervis, an Ecuadorian naturalist and writer, tracing Humboldt's path along the southern slope of Antisana. The path crosses haciendas that have changed little since Humboldt's time, indeed since the Spanish arrival and the collapse of the Inca empire. Conditions on the haciendas remain feudal. The workers, mostly of Indian descent, do not own their land or even their houses and may be expelled at the whim of the *hidalgo*.

The tension between serf and *hidalgo* is as old as the New World. South of here, in the valleys near Cuzco, Peru, the Indians have ritualized the relationship. Having clung to their

own cosmology quite independently of the European tradition and recognizing parts of the constellation Scorpio as *El Contor* (the Inca word for "vulture," from which the Spanish word *condor* is derived), the Indians envision the bird as a symbol of themselves. Appropriately, they regard the bull as a symbol of the *conquistador*. In a grisly ceremony echoing these painful images, the Indians sew the feet of a condor into the haunch of a bull, and over the course of the night the animals are left to torture each other, the condor lacerating the bull's shoulder and the bull rolling on the ground in an attempt to crush its tormentor. If at dawn the condor is still living, it is released.

María Helena and I cling to the flanks of Antisana, covered with a verdigris of green lichens, on a trail that seems etched into the sky. The crashing river below is almost inaudible.

Sheep-grazed paramo on the flanks of Antisana.

The armed rosette of a puya bromeliad.

Ahead the valley flattens into paramo. A few tattered clouds batter the earth, and for most of the day there is no sound other than the shearing wind. The coarse grass here has neither the softness of the *páramo de lluvia* nor its diversity. Five thousand sheep graze this pasture in the sky. Twenty generations of *hidalgos* have seeded the paramo with Eurasian and African grasses as alien as the sheep that eat them: *pasto miel, pasto janéiro, pasto alemán, pasto dallis,* and *kikuyo* (kikuyu grass, the same species that has strangled much of lowland Hawaii). There is a terrible and yet heroic cultural imperative here. The seeding of exotic grasses and their management by cattle and sheep are more art than mere agronomy. This generational devotion slowly transforms the landscape into something resembling ancestral Iberia. Like concepts of beauty, these traditions are nearly impossible to tease out of the fabric of culture. What an ecologist perceives as a subdued land, devoid of diversity, is an earthly paradise to a *haciendero*.

The sheep have been here so long that nobody remembers what the original vegetation was like. The paramo is a place of survivors. There are toxic sedges, a few hunching cushion plants, bent yellow daisies, which present the lowest possible profile to the grazers, and silicon-reinforced tussock grasses, which act like vegetable millstones to wear down their teeth. Here are the armed rosettes of the *puya* bromeliads, whose white-flowering stalks are as tall as a man. Their leaves bear recurved teeth as sharp as fishhooks. Today the *puyas* are in flower; they blossom only once, then die. The spectacled bears, which are almost extinct now on Antisana, are reported to sit next to a puya and eat it petal by petal, the way a Frenchman eats an artichoke.

Humboldt's hut still stands somewhere on this paramo. Nearby, the Fundación Antisana has built another stone house, where schoolchildren from Quito are taken to see condors. Above the hut is the snow-marbled basaltic lava plug of Antisana, eroded to a few jagged pinnacles. The meltwater from its glaciers accumulates in the Laguna de Mica, which covers only a half square mile and is a flawless mirror for the mountain. We have crossed the Continental Divide. The lake is one of the sources of the Amazon, spawning a cold, shallow stream as clear as the air, which slides east from the wetlands.

Francisco de Orellana and Gonzalo Pizarro, standing somewhere near this spot in 1541, noted the water's strange eastward trajectory and decided to follow its course into the forest below. It was a massive endeavor. On February 21, Pizarro force-marched 350 *hidalgos* (each in metal armor), 2,000 attack dogs, 4,000 Indian bearers, 2,000 pack-bearing llamas, and 2,000 swine into a snowy mountain valley east of Quito. The account is not clear, but it may be that the valley María Helena and I have followed today, beneath the ivory alpine slopes of Antisana, was the explorers' gateway to the Amazon lowlands. The animals, unaccustomed to the tropical heat, all died. Most of the men (including Pizarro) soon turned back. But Orellana and a handful of others had traveled so far that they were forced to complete the journey, rafting down the Amazon to the Atlantic through the earth's greatest wilderness.

Today the Laguna de Mica is broad and shallow, its margins fringed by mud flats and plains of rushes. It smells mildly of decomposition. A black-necked stilt is monotonously complaining in the short reeds, and a ruddy turnstone is keening in the mud. An ovenbird, as brown as the wind-blown grasses, searches for seeds among the tussocks near the lake. When it descends, it puffs up in midair, an air brake of distended and chaotic feathers that drops lightly to earth.

After a long search of the air above an umber facade of columnar lava, María Helena and I spot two brown juvenile condors floating on updrafts, the tips of their primaries splayed like uplifted fingers. They navigate by tipping their bodies ever so slightly into, and then away from, the wind. When they alight, the condors are exactly the color of the rock face, but their aeries, atop overhanging promontories, are marked by cascades of white scats.

Condors are vultures, carrion-eaters. Once they subsisted on the abundant carcasses of llamas and alpacas. Today this sterile plain has once again become an ideal condor habitat. The birds scarf up the corpses of the alien animals that have so transmuted the environment since the Spanish arrival. They depend especially on stillborn calves and lambs. Like the *puya* and the sedges, the condors have become survivors. In the Western eye these birds are the symbol of Andean wilderness, and in the imagination of the Indian, of freedom. Today both wilderness and freedom are illusions. The condors are, in fact, the symbol of a demolished land, one of the first outposts of Europe in the New World.

Mbaracayú

A Relict in Time

WE SPRINT IN THE GLOWERING FOREST, among the startling columns of afternoon light, hunting for armadillos. Most of the light has already departed the understory, although crowns of the trees are illuminated above. My hosts, Ty Kuangí, Tatunamh'llangi, and Kaju Pukungi, are as fleet and silent as brocket deer. I have a hard time keeping up, for I am carrying Pua'ayi (*pua' ayi* is the Aché word for capuchin monkey), a four-year old girl. They are looking for the armadillos' telltale holes and so far have investigated many a dry well.

Ty Kuangí, Tatunamh'llangi, and Kaju Pukungi are Aché Indians, hunter-gatherers who live in the forest of Mbaracayú, a nature reserve in northeastern Paraguay. The name of the place means "yellow maraca" in Guaraní, referring to the ukulele-like instrument characteristic of the tribe; legend tells of an Indian minstrel who wandered through the forest playing a maraca crafted of yellow wood. For these men Mbaracayú is the universe, and hunting is the only way of life they know. Yet the forest is only 65,587 acres, about three times the size of New York's Central Park. There are no trails in the northern part of Mbaracayú. The Aché walk through the closed forest, keeping in touch with each other with shouts that mimic the sounds made by animals. They memorize the shapes of the tree crowns. The Aché have more than ten names for these shapes, and by memorizing their order, use them to navigate through a forest that would seem featureless to the uninitiated.

Often whole families go on these trips, which last from a few hours, like this afternoon jaunt to get a snack for dinner, or as long as fifty days. Their catch is usually cooked and eaten where it is killed. Although the Aché are proficient at using bows and arrows and spears, my companions are hunting without weapons. They also disdain hammocks, preferring to sleep on the forest floor. Living off the land, an Aché hunting party leaves home with nothing and returns with nothing.

*Beetle larvae in an
Aché cooking pot.*

In a light gap made by a treefall, Ty Kuarangí, Kaju Pukungi, and Tatunamh'llangi stop for a bit of carbohydrate loading. Six weeks earlier they pushed down a palm tree in this clearing. Wood decays quickly in the constant humidity of Mbaracayú, and today the rotten core of the trunk is full of weevil larvae. Ty Kuarangí pries a weevil grub, about four inches long, from the fibrous, vinegar-yeast-scented palm heart and pops it into his mouth, spitting out only its brown head. He offers one to Pua'ayi and me. I chew it quickly to stop its squirming. It has a winy, sour taste. Pua'ayi gobbles hers down, sucking on the empty skin like a lollipop, and asks for more.

The men hunt mostly with their ears and their noses. They listen for the shuffle of an armadillo in the leaf litter, the bustle of a tapir. Tatunamh'llangi can follow the path of a tapir for kilometers just by its musky aroma. At last Ty Kuarangí spots a nine-banded armadillo ducking into its burrow in a low patch of broad-leaved *Marantus*. He understands armadillo psychology, knows they are lazy. Protected by dermal plates, armadillos have little to fear and drop their guard easily. Ty Kuarangí knows that most armadillos construct a shallow chamber, a front porch so to speak, near the entrance to their burrows, where they will wait until danger passes without expending the energy to descend into the labyrinth below. Ty Kuarangí shoves his bare foot into the hole just beneath the chamber. He predicted correctly; the armadillo is trapped, unable to flee to safety above or below. He reaches into the burrow and, with his thumb, snaps the armadillo's neck. It lurches out, thrashing, and takes a few long minutes to die. Everybody is pleased. Armadillo meat, baked in an open fire in its shell, tastes like roast lamb.

*

An Aché hunter digging for an armadillo.

50

With no seacoast, Paraguay has remained isolated from the rest of South America. The isolation has endowed the country with a certain charm: Asunción, the capital, has the atmosphere and pace of a city in the 1950s. Traditionally only one conduit of commerce, the Paraguay River, linked the country with the exterior. The river is highly seasonal, exceeding its banks during the summer and contracting to a sandbar-snarled trickle in the winter. Even in this age of roads and trucks, the river is filled with lazy barges pushed by tugboats during the rainy, high-water season. The Paraguay River divides the country into the largely deserted Chaco, which extends west all the way to the foothills of the Andes in Bolivia, and the densely populated east. Only 3 percent of the population lives in the Chaco, on 60 percent of the land. The Chaco is sandy, the remnant of an ancient sea bottom, and its soil is fragile and poorly drained. It has the aspect of a green ocean where the vault of sky seems to overwhelm the earth. Lakes that look like mud puddles punctuate the land, expanding and contracting seasonally. Where the plain is crumpled by river valleys, it supports forest. The alluvial sand gives the trees the necessary drainage to set their roots, and the rough terrain affords protection from the woodcutters. On still nights in the Chaco, you can occasionally hear the maned wolves howling to the heavens. Leggy and tall, they are adapted to the open grassland, but now they have invaded the alien and closed forest, an expansion of niche necessitated by the burning of the savanna.

Eastern Paraguay, by contrast, was once densely forested right to the Atlantic. As in the west, the only way to enter this dark wilderness was by river. The Spanish and Portuguese explorers, and the Jesuits who followed them, called this the Bosque Atlantico, or Atlantic woods. At first they colonized the river margins, using fire to make small clearings, and over the centuries they proceeded to cut down most of the forest in southwestern Brazil and eastern Paraguay, converting it to pasture for cattle. The cattle brought their own ecosystem; their hooves cut the soil and their hides carried the hitchhiking seeds of the Eurasian grasses that they ate — species that were adapted to colonizing disturbed soils.

These subtropical forests are like no other on earth. Several times during the past quarter million years, they were connected to the Amazonian forest, but for the past seventy or eighty thousand years they have been isolated from that font of diversity six hundred miles north. The Bosque Atlantico, therefore, has most of the genera of Amazonia, but the species, through long isolation, are different. As a biologist who is familiar with the Amazon, I perceive many familiar motifs in this forest, but the details are different. Time and distance are all that it takes to change the species — and a bit of chill. During the winter, there are frequent cold nights when cyclonic storms blow north from Antarctica, and these episodes have distilled the full diversity of Amazonia into a few hardy survivors in each genus. Temperate species have also mixed with tropical ones in the Bosque Atlantico, and many species are at the limit of their range, just hanging on.

*

Slashed and burned pasture on the edge of Mbaracayú.

These are the last wild moments in the Bosque Atlantico. Today, only 8 percent of the forest in Paraguay remains, almost all of it in Mbaracayú . By 2015 Paraguay will be an importer of wood (now it's an exporter, mostly illegally to Brazil). The adjoining Brazilian state of Paraná, except for the reserve around Iguazú Falls, is deforested. The cattle ranches, like the small swiddens of the Ecuadorian *ceja*, begin with immolation of the forest, and the first generation of cattle graze among charred stumps. The few trees that survive in the cleared zone bear the contortions and deviations of habit; crooked trunks and angled boughs — the very distortions that the Aché once memorized on their hunts. These isolated forms hint of what the canopy was once like, but tell no more. The trees never return and are replaced by a striking green plain, punctuated by the occasional forest giant. After deforestation the snaking arroyos dry up and the land loses its capacity to retain water. The forest-eating cattle move like a plague of caterpillars munching through a tomato garden. Brazil and Paraguay are sacrificing their futures for a giant *churrasco* (barbecue) today.

52

The Bosque Atlantico in Mbaracayú.

As in Ecuador, the aesthetics of cattle ranching have a cultural component. This is the land of the caballero, the romantic cowboy who is an avatar of the Iberian desert. Romantic and proud, perhaps, but he does not have an easy life. The caballero, clad in leather chaps and triangular leather hat, lives in a diminished ecosystem of his own making. He shares his house and garden with his cattle, among flies, ticks, and massive amounts of manure.

The northern border of Mbaracayú is the Brazilian frontier. Two parallel roads, one Brazilian and one Paraguayan and both as straight as lines drawn on a map, run along the frontier. The edge of the reserve, and of Paraguay, is as distinct as an Australian rabbit fence: a wall of Paraguayan forest fronting a horizon of Brazilian pasture. There are no customs checkpoints on the border with Brazil, but the *guarda-bosques* (forest rangers) carry side arms. Brazilian tree rustlers, driving flatbed trucks known as *rodeiros*, smuggle logs from Mbaracayú across the undefended border with near impunity. Today a Brazilian truck has become stuck in the mud, and its antsy crew is being detained at gunpoint by the rangers. Most of the damage to the reserve is more subtle. Hot winds from the pasture penetrate a long way into the boundary of the reserve, fostering a bramble of secondary plants like those that would grow in a treefall or at the edge of a road. This phenomenon, known as the edge effect, is so pronounced that it creates changes in the flowering and fruiting time of the trees, creating what are essentially ecological orphans that reproduce out of phase with the rest of their species.

When Mbaracayú Forest Nature Reserve was founded, just after the 1989 coup, the government mandated that all lands considered "unproductive" — including the last patches of the Bosque Atlantico — were to be converted to pasture. At the time only 15 percent of the original forest remained, and most was badly fragmented. The Mbaracayú Reserve was established in an imaginative manner, uniting a rich and a poor nation in defense of biological diversity and the rights of indigenous people. The effort was initiated by the International Financial Corporation, which had acquired the land through default on a loan, and coordinated by the Nature Conservancy and the Fundación Moisés Bertoni. Two million dollars of the purchase price was provided by the AES/Barbers Point Company, which generates electricity for Oahu, Hawaii. To meet the rising demand for electricity in Hawaii, the company had built a new coal-burning power plant, which was expected to release 14.4 million tons of carbon, mostly in the form of carbon dioxide, into the atmosphere over its thirty-five-year life. Acknowledging that this carbon would inevitably contribute to the global greenhouse effect, the utility company promised to compensate for its pollution by preventing the release of an equivalent amount of carbon into the atmosphere. It chose to conserve the carbon locked up in the living biomass of the Mbaracayú Reserve, which would have been released as the inevitable consequence of burning the forest and converting it to pasture. In fact, quantitative inventories have showed that more than twice that amount, approximately 29 million tons of carbon, are sequestered in the reserve.

Some 87 percent of the reserve is forested; the rest consists of sinuous intrusions of savanna and lakes — a pattern opposite that of the Chaco. Although statuesque, with trees exceeding 150 feet in height, the forest of Mbaracayú is relatively depauperate; one quarter of an acre contained only eighty-five species of trees and shrubs — rich by temperate standards, but poor compared to the two or three hundred species that would be expected in that size plot in the Amazon. Many of the trees at Mbaracayú are deciduous, an adaptation to the distinct seasons of Paraguay. Many are interwoven with vines, so when one tree falls, it usually drags several others down with it. Vinyness, at least in the New World tropics and subtropics, is a sure indicator of past disturbance, and although Mbaracayú has never been converted to pasture, it has, over the centuries, been disturbed piecemeal.

The traces of human presence are everywhere. Honeybees, which were brought to Paraguay by the Jesuits, have escaped and gone feral. In recent years they have hybridized with angry African bees; the offspring retain the gene for anger. Swarms of Africanized bees have been known to attack a human or an animal fifty yards away; most, fortunately, are docile.

The Mbaracayú forest, even in remote areas, is filled with wild orange trees. Native to China, oranges were almost certainly brought to Paraguay by the Jesuits, who had encountered the fruit in their journeys to the coast of China. The nearest Jesuit mission is one hundred twenty miles from Mbaracayú, on the banks of the Paraná River. The mission was destroyed in the mid-1600s, but by then the oranges had already escaped. In four hundred years they spread at a rate of over a mile per year. Unlike the plants introduced to the Hawaiian Islands or the pastures of Ecuador, the oranges do not dominate the local forest. Instead they have become assimilated into the mosaic of native species. They have retained their Asian phenology, producing fruit at times when the native trees don't. The local peccaries, pacas, howler monkeys, and capuchin monkeys have come to depend on the oranges, and this no doubt accounts for their rapid dispersal. In fact, because of the oranges, the Bosque Atlantico today may be able to support more of these animals than the pre-Columbian forest did.

As in Ecuador, the main treasures for the Spanish conquerors were botanical. The Jesuits

Wild oranges.

noted that the local Guaraní Indians were enthusiastically sipping yerba maté, a pungent tea brewed from the shiny, scalloped leaves of a forest tree, a kind of holly. At the time Paraguay had a monopoly on its production. Having themselves rapidly become maté aficionados, the Jesuits began exporting the dried leaves of the plant to Spain, where maté became hugely popular and hugely profitable. Maté competed with cocoa, another New World plant, and with coffee and tea from the Old World to become the chic social beverage of the newly established cafés of European cities. All four plants contain either caffeine or closely related alkaloids, which had evolved to kill insect pests but which also happen to be exhilarating to humans. The Europeans had never experienced anything like them — drinks that animated the body and provoked lively conversation. By the middle 1500s, maté had become the preferred beverage in much of Europe. If the supply of maté had persisted, very likely most of the world today would drink it rather than coffee and tea. However, in an effort to elevate the price of the beverage, the Paraguayan Jesuits squeezed off its supply and prevented the export of the young plants beyond the borders of the colony. The Europeans turned to the cheaper alternatives and in time lost their maté habit. The export market never recovered, but the domestic market flourished, and maté tea, mixed with fragrant mango leaves, continues to be the beverage of choice in Uruguay, Argentina, southern Brazil, and Paraguay.

In the forest of Mbaracayú, wild maté is everywhere, and as with the orange trees, its commonness may be due to enrichment of the forest by centuries of human activity. Itinerant Aché maté harvesters rove through the reserve, setting up camps here and there for a week or so, collecting and drying the wild leaves.

A rectangular island of forest surrounded by pasture, Mbaracayú is the last refuge in Paraguay for many of the species of the Bosque Atlantico. Approximately 413 species of birds occur on the reserve; 16 percent of them are in danger of extinction. Especially threatened are the purple-winged ground dove and the black-necked biatas, which are adapted to the relictual bamboo forests in the center of the reserve. With no remaining stands of bamboo for hundreds of miles they can no longer migrate, so they live on a virtual island. The big edible birds, especially the black-fronted piping guan, rosette-winged spadebill, and vinaceous-breasted parrot, were the first to become rare. The forest also supports maned wolves (which stick to the fingers of savanna that insinuate the forest), tapirs, jaguars, giant otters, collared anteaters, giant armadillos (which grow to more than a yard long), and bush dogs, whose orphaned puppies are occasionally adopted by the Aché.

Just after dawn I sit, rock-still, in a clearing next to a cluster of bamboos, bromeliads, and orchids on the edge of the smooth and silent river. Immediately I notice the nuances, the language of the forest. A tiptoeing agouti, like a tripping quadruped ballerina, appears in a slanting shaft of sunlight. The bamboos, which by bending can withstand the twisting water, are like a crafted Chinese garden, a still life in which even the reflection of green water on jointed stems is carefully planned. Next to me is a pile of wet tapir scats, flecked with undigested orange seeds. A flock of skittery sulfur butterflies have alighted on them, dipping their proboscises into the delicious lode of nutrients; the females are building eggs and need these rarities. It is slightly chilly this morning; a heliconid butterfly — red, black, and yellow, with red ocelli, like false eyes, on the inside wings — spreads its wings, even its antennae, to capture the sun's warmth. It is expressing pheromones — a sexual attractant — from waxy extrusions on its abdomen. Warmed and volatilized by the sun, the pheromones invisibly coil through the forest. In a column of warm sunlight a blue and yellow flux of gnats seems like an animate rainbow.

Lyre-winged heliconid and tiny nymphalid butterflies at a mineral excrescence.

In closed forest like this, one observes first with one's ears, an imperative that the Aché taught me during the armadillo hunt. It is so still that I can hear the clicking of the armored legs of a column of army ants raiding a nearby log, and the snapping of a swallow-tailed hesperid butterfly skipping among the canopies of the flooded trees. Two tinamous are piping forlornly, at opposite points of the compass. I spot one of them, on the highest branch of a dead tree; its red dewlap seems incandescent in the bright sunlight. A family of macaws is shrieking somewhere in the darkling river valley; an invisible toucan is yipping like a puppy; a trilling flock of parakeets passes nearby and then retreats into the silence; a kingfisher shouts a startling staccato chatter a microsecond before it dips from its perch and splashes into the river. Two bare-throated bellbirds patrol the leafless treetops on either side of the river. They are obviously very agitated, hopping back and forth between the branches, inflating their purple-skinned throats and tossing angry *gongs* across the clearing.

Mbaracayú is also the last outpost of the Aché; 16,000 acres of the reserve were set aside as the exclusive property of the tribe. They have inherited a diminished place, but it's a lot better than nothing. And it is still largely wild. Last week a jaguar and her cub circled a rangers' camp in the Sierra de Amambai, the range of buttes on the eastern edge of the reserve where there are waterfalls 180 feet high. She prowled around the camp all night long and once approached a sleeping man, screaming and switching her tail. Two rangers stood guard, while the other three slept.

The Aché settlement of Jejui'mi is a few ramshackle huts on the moth-eaten western edge of the forest in a swidden of bananas and cecropia trees. It is in uneasy proximity to Villa Ygatimi, where the colonists live. Isolated by culture and language from the majority indigenous tribe, the Guaraní, and from the Spanish settlers, the Aché have never had a comfortable relationship with outsiders. According to some accounts the Spanish forced the tribe into slavery — harvesting maté, cutting wood, and squeezing essence from oranges — a subjugation that has persisted, without the formal imprimatur of slavery, into this century. The tribe's only recourse was to retreat into the shrinking forest and to live by their traditional means of hunting and gathering. But the forest has never been generous, even to its own. In fact, it's a hostile place: nearly one in ten Aché hunters was killed by jaguars. When things got tough, the Aché would raid the nearby ranches, stealing crops and killing cattle and horses. They became fringe-dwellers, on the edge of the forest and of Western society. The colonists retaliated by placing a bounty on the Aché, and organized manhunts continued into the 1980s.

Hunters stalked and killed Aché men like game animals, kidnapping the women and children and selling them into prostitution and slavery.

In spite of the trauma of exploitation, the Aché maintain an ebullient curiosity about outsiders. Yet the exigencies of life in the forest have forced the Aché to make brutal adaptations. There are no words in their language for hello, thanks, or good-bye. Theirs is a small population. Everyone is familiar with everyone else, yet this is a terrible place to have no relatives, for the Aché tradition is to abandon those who are injured or orphaned in the forest. Kaju Pukungi, whose mother died when he was a child and whose father subsequently denied him, has lived from hearth to hearth since he was a teenager. Now thirty, he moves on when people get tired of his acculturated ways.

An Aché child.

Until 1978, a small group of Aché inside what is now Mbaracayú Reserve had never had contact with outsiders. They avoided the savannas, the haunts of their traditional enemies, the Guaraní. After contact, they were expelled from the forest and forced to settle in agricultural communities. In one generation they made the transition from hunting and gathering to agriculture that had taken the ancestors of the colonists a millennium. Where once they used to cut down trees to collect wild honey, they now became beekeepers. Inevitably, the transplanted Aché were decimated by disease and hunger. When the reserve was established in 1992, there were no Aché left in Mbaracayú forest; all were living on the margins of the colonist settlements.

Today the Aché once again are permitted to hunt in the reserve, a privilege not shared (at least on paper) by the colonists. When well monitored, hunting is a form of sustainable extraction that is no more damaging than the harvest of maté leaves. The essential question has become how much hunting the reserve can sustain without depleting the populations of animals that it was designed to support.

I awaken at 5:50 under a *luna menguante* (waning moon) and watch the morning seep into the Villa Ygatimi (the name means "small white canoe" in Guaraní). Outside, a cold thunderstorm is perched over the pastures that spread in every direction from Villa Ygatimi. The village is tidy and clean, red dirt roads with a few errant cows and bulls, dusty red cement sidewalks, and red tile roofs. There are pretty parks with shading orange trees. The roosters and humans are already awake; the village dogs are still sleeping on various dry porches, tails draped over their noses to conserve heat. Three cowboys, wrapped in ponchos, are riding their sleepy horses to work. A kiskadee, onomatopoeically known in Guaraní as a

59

pitowe, is declaring its cosmos from a treetop. I am sitting in the kitchen of Doña Helena, who is preparing breakfast, frying succulent slabs of bacon. Raw milk, still warm from the cow, is dreamily steaming in the chill morning air. She prepares a gourd of maté. "The *campesinos,*" she explains, "can lack meat, sugar, milk . . . but never maté." An evangelist preacher is blabbing from a radio near the kitchen, in a dark corner where mysteries dwell. Somewhere nearby, another radio is playing an accordion polka.

Already the distant burr of a sawmill can be heard, and the air is filling with the tannic aroma of cut timber. In eastern Paraguay, no sanctuary can exist without regard to the imperatives of the local economy. Clearly, alternatives to hunting and tree-rustling had to be found that would provide a sustainable living for the burgeoning population of colonists that had settled on all sides of the reserve. Personnel from the Fundación Moisés Bertoni established committees and cooperatives to expand productivity and to integrate the local economy with wider markets. Each committee has about twelve families, and fifteen committees comprise one cooperative. Integral to their organization is the involvement of the local women. While the colonists used to scrap among themselves, the new enterprises embrace the generous frontier tradition of *hacer mingas* (barn raising). For the first time, schools have been built for the committee members, but the necessary equipment — pencils, books, uniforms — is too expensive for many parents, and in the familial economy of Villa Ygatimi, children are often needed to work the fields from March to May. Many remain uneducated.

The committees produce and market commodities such as chickens and onions. The Comité Tendal is typical, dedicated to an enterprise traditional to Paraguay and to Mbaracayú: maté production. Seeds taken from the reserve and from old plantations are germinated and grown to seedlings, then distributed to homesteads throughout the area. Maté seedlings require understory shade, a resource that is in short supply on the denuded plain. At the Comité Tendal they are grown under the artificial shade of palm thatch. About a thousand maté trees have been distributed to each family, a resource of considerable value, given that two pounds of leaves is worth about one U.S. dollar. It takes a plant five years to produce seed, but its leaves may be harvested before then, and a typical tree has thirty to fifty years of productivity. In the forest, wild maté trees grow 36 to 45 feet high, with straight trunks that make it hard to harvest their leaves. But on the plantations they are groomed and pruned like bonsai trees and coppiced to a height of only 4 to 12 feet. The Comité Tendal is planning to construct a maté factory soon to retain the added value resulting from processing at Mbaracayú rather than exporting it to Asunción.

Having contented neighbors means safety for the Aché and for the last scrap of Paraguayan Bosque Atlantico. Economic decline would place irresistible pressure on this last great place. Here development is conservation. The Aché have returned to their natal forest, although their universe has shrunk to a few hundred square miles and their culture has diminished. Already some of their oldest traditions exist only in legend and story. But, like the wattled bellbird gonging to its neighbor, they survive in the forest they know. The lunar pastures — Iberia transplanted — are, for the moment, held at bay.

Cultivated yerba maté seedlings.

Guaraqueçaba

Island of the Ice Age

A LAND-WIND. The sea is crumpled by the troubling and scented zephyrs from the shore. At dawn the sea is as dark and bruised as the sky, which has been shedding tufts of rain all night long on Guaraqueçaba, a ramshackle village on the edge of the Baía de Laranjeiras (Bay of the Orange Trees — as in Mbaracayú, wild orange trees, introduced by Iberian pioneers a half millennium ago, are common on the islands in the bay). Three Magellanic penguins, vagrants from the coast of Patagonia and the Malvinas, have washed up dead on the mud beach in front of town. The sky belongs to the frigate birds, which on this glowering morning are in the low clouds. By midmorning the weather has broken, but the sun lingers behind the hills, denying the early hummingbirds and bluebottle flies its warmth. The flies wait a little longer, perched on twig and sill until, blessed by the light, they abruptly flick into the air, then alight on the flotsam on the muddy shore. The hummingbirds, twisting and straining on the wing, insert their bills into the still-closed corollas of red hibiscus.

The Baía de Laranjeiras is rimmed by a dark brow of mangroves. Above is the shadowed Serra do Mar, a vast range of tropical forested mountains, and above them the angry clouds, torn by the winds that race through the mountain valleys and tousle the bay. Fog covers the lowest hills, creating the illusion that some of the high peaks are floating in air. The coastal mountains, like those on Moloka'i, grab the sea-wind and distill its moisture. They present dramatic facades to the sea: leaping vistas and jagged ranges that challenge the eye. Silhouetted against the western sun, the peaks and crests look like waves on a lumpy, stormy sea: surreal, like Japanese silk paintings. At sunset one can see every tree etched on the mountain ridges.

Opposite page: Aerial view of mangroves among meandering ocean channels.

The Baía de Laranjeiras and the foothills of the Serra do Mar.

The Serra do Mar comprises the largest continuous patch of Brazil's Mata Atlântica, the coastal forest that once extended from the state of Santa Catarina, south of Guaraqueçaba, to tropical Bahia, 600 miles north. Once connected to the Amazon forest, but today separated from it by an arid intrusion of savanna and brittle *cerrado* forest, the Mata Atlântica has evolved in isolation from its huge western neighbor for at least 70,000 years. As in Mbaracayú, the species are all variations on themes of Amazonia. Almost all of the genera of Amazonian trees, birds, mammals, and invertebrates are found in the forest, but the species are new. The diversity is extraordinary. Small areas of forest in the state of Bahia have a richness of flowering plant species that is greater than almost anywhere else on earth: one survey conducted there counted 458 species of flowering plants in slightly less than 2.5 acres. That's about half as many species as are found in the entire state of New York, and more than any Amazonian sample of comparable size east of the Andean *ceja de la montaña*.

But here in southern Brazil, the subtropical forests of the Serra do Mar, like those of Mbaracayú, are low-growing and impoverished in species compared to their counterparts to the north. Their low diversity is misleading, however, because of the region's high rate of endemism. Of the woody plant species of the Serra do Mar, 53 percent occur nowhere else on earth. If the forest is destroyed, these species will become extinct. And it is more than just the plants that are unique and threatened. In 1992 a new monkey species — one of four species of *Micro-leão*, nocturnal marmosets as small as hamsters, which live in the treetops — was discovered on Ilha de Superaguí, the barrier island that comprises the eastern shore of the Baía de Laranjeiras. On a planet dominated by primates, the discovery was an event noted around the world.

A diurnal tufted-ear marmoset.

Today, less than 5 percent of the Mata Atlântica remains uncut, the rest sacrificed to cacao, lumber, and urbanization. The surviving forest has been severely fragmented, mostly into pieces less than ten acres in size that are insufficient to sustain populations of large animals and trees. The lowland forests around the Baía de Laranjeiras are typical of this decline. In 1970 a narrow dirt road was bashed through the coastal forest to Guaraqueçaba from Antonina, at the base of the Serra do Mar. Until then Guaraqueçaba had been isolated by the mountains, accessible only by means of an occasional itinerant coastal vessel trading among the settlements of the islands in the bay. Today the road ambles across a denuded plain of pasture and scruffy *capoeira* (secondary growth) through prosperous *fazendas* (plantations) and shantytowns erected near sawmills. A few straggling *juçara* palms, strung along the river courses, are all that remain of the lowland forest that once nudged the sea. Asian water buffaloes, which have broad hooves able to withstand the soggy ground and even occasional inundation, are the cash cows here. Their arrival was followed by that of the ubiquitous cattle egrets; one is perched on the back of a buffalo in classic egret posture. As in Ecuador and Paraguay, it is Iberia transplanted: a bovine monotony. Regardless, the rivers run clear — a sign of health in the watershed (although the burden of pesticides they carry, in a nation where DDT is still legal, may be another story). The rivers still have substantial populations of broad-nosed caimans and provide nurseries for fish and shrimp; during the summer rainy season, from December to February, flotillas of blue crabs migrate to the sea to spawn.

Guará means scarlet ibis in Guaraní. Centuries ago, during the summer, the ibises used to nest by the thousands in the tallest trees, converting whole forests to a crimson that could be seen for miles across the bay. Roseate spoonbills nested alongside the ibises, complementing their aerial rookeries with buffy pink. But the birds that gave the village its name are now extinct in littoral Paraná, and spoonbills are uncommon. Regardless, 330 species of birds, both marine and terrestrial, have survived in the bay and its surrounding mountains. Many are endemic and some, like the black-fronted piping guan, survive only in vestigial numbers. This furtive denizen of the interior *terra firme* forests is heard more often than seen; its plaintive descending note seems to imbue the understory with melancholy.

Founded in 1545, Guaraqueçaba was the first city in the state of Paraná. Its balustraded waterfront reflects the town's former glory, however brief. The Portuguese pilgrims and their African slaves took the land from the resident Tupinambá Indians, who had been farming the lowlands and fishing in the Baía de Laranjeiras for centuries. History does not record whether the conquest was peaceful or whether the Indians succumbed to the usual mélange of Western diseases. However, the array of physiognomies among the region's modern inhabitants, who are known as Caiçaras, testifies that the three cultures — indigenous, African, and European — readily intermixed.

Guaraqueçaba was soon eclipsed by the deep-water port of Paranaguá, twelve miles south, and was relegated to desultory isolation for nearly three centuries. In the mid-nineteenth century, Swiss immigrants under the leadership of one William Michaud, a utopian dreamer, founded an agricultural commune on Ilha de Superaguí and on Ilha do Mel, in the lee of the barrier island. Superaguí, with its empty, storm-tossed beach 25 miles long, is a place of illusion. Though riotously green, it lacks fresh water for agriculture. The colonies inevitably failed, their crops succumbing to thirst and salt spray. The moldering ruins of Michaud's experiment, entwined in pink-flowering railroad vine, persist today. Only the hardy Caiçaras managed to hang on, but just barely, extracting a living from the sea and the forest.

During the centuries that Guaraqueçaba stagnated, the coastal forests of Brazil, from Bahia to Santa Catarina, burned. The Mata Atlântica was utterly fragmented, reduced to an archipelago of small forest plots surrounded by cropland and cities. Much of the destruction was directly related to the fateful decision of the Paraguayan Jesuits to restrict the trade of yerba maté leaves, forcing Europeans to switch to cocoa and coffee. The northern lowlands of the Mata Atlântica were ideal for cacao (itself from the Amazonian lowlands), and the mountainous forests of the southern coast, where sea-borne rains and cool winds soothed the nights, were perfect for coffee (from the Ethiopian highlands). By the early 1800s, the finest coffee in the world was coming from southern Brazil, and powerful commercial empires were being built on cacao in the northeast. Sugar, used to sweeten the new beverages and to manufacture rum, likewise was an empire-builder, and the last scraps of forest were converted to sugar cane. Brazil became rich, but these economies had debilitating social consequences. All of these crops are labor-intensive, and slave labor was integral to their success; this economic imperative may explain why slavery was abolished in Brazil only in 1888, later than any other country in the Americas except Cuba (another sugar and coffee producer).

By 1937 there were only 9,500 Caiçaras. Today the population is approximately the same, but with the arrival of the road and of modern medicine, it is growing fast. The average Caiçara family has five children. They live in fifty-eight small villages, each comprising a few extended families, scattered among the islands of the Baía de Laranjeiras. Reliant on fishing and the modest agriculture that the salty soils permit, the people are humble but proud. The mean income in 1994 was equivalent to $370; by contrast the mean income for Brazil as a whole was $2,100. The Caiçaras are largely uneducated. Only five certified teachers live in the entire region. Their jobs are considered hardship posts. Even if more teachers could be found, the government could not afford to send one to each village. As in Mbaracayú, the road changed everything, bringing commerce, a modicum of public health, and educational opportunities, but also destruction, not just to the Mata Atlântica, but to the Caiçara way of life. The road attracted politicians and especially missionaries, bringing the traditional Catholic faith as well as nine Protestant sects. Today there are more churches than schools.

On this winter weekend, Guaraqueçaba is full of tourists from Curitiba and São Paulo. I got one of the last rooms in town, for the equivalent of four dollars per night, at Dona Mariana's pousada, on a street lined with mango trees fronting the sea. It is full of young men clad in newly washed shirts, preening for the dance tonight. My bed is an old wooden crate, with a board that rubs my spine when I sleep on my back. The shuttered window faces an open sewer that drains into the bay. Down the hall is the communal bath. The shower stands in a pool of soapy water. Someone's damp T-shirt hangs from the door; blinded by soapy water, I grab it to wipe my face.

The Guaraqueçabans seem confused by the intrusion of urbanites. The tourists, of course, bring money. But as they flash it, they remind young people that there is a more prosperous, glamorous life outside the village. Today the locals are sullen and don't even respond when greeted with a cheerful "boa tarde!" Last evening, as I walked down the street back to the pousada, people clicked their doors shut, one by one.

*

After the road was built, forest that had once been inaccessible, and therefore a virtual commons, suddenly became valuable property. Timber, which once had no way to reach market, was easily trucked out of the newly violated forest. But the greatest peril to the region may have been the proximity of the road to Brazil's burgeoning urban centers. Wealthy urbanites from Curitiba and São Paulo cut up the lowlands into *fazendas*. The land, only a few yards above sea level, was not conducive to large-scale agriculture. By the 1990s 70 percent of the coastal plain had been converted to small-scale pasture for water buffalo.

Next to raising buffalo, the easiest route to wealth in the lowlands lay in the *juçara* palm. The spindly *juçara*, which crowds river courses throughout Brazil, is a signature species of the floodplain. Its profuse black fruits, rich in carbohydrates and iron, in other parts of Brazil are macerated to make a healthful drink or a flavoring for ice cream. Its flavor is unlike that of any other fruit on earth: a mixture of pears and Kaopectate. However, instead of harvesting the jaçara fruits in the traditional manner, the colonists took the plant's succulent, folded embryonic leaves, known as *palmito* (literally, "little palm," but the translation is inevitably "heart of palm"). Fresh or bottled in brine, *palmito* had become a popular middle-class food in Brazil's urban centers, as well as a luxury treat with snob appeal in foreign markets. But it's a costly treat, because the entire tree must be destroyed to extract *palmito*. Even so, *juçara* grow in clumps of three to fifteen trunks, and as long as one trunk is spared, the cluster will regenerate in a few years and may be harvested anew. If managed in a sustainable manner, the *juçara* could have provided long-term employment for the unskilled Caiçaras. But the factory owners kept the prices paid to them low, forcing them to cut as many palms as possible to make ends meet; none were spared. By 1992 the three processing plants for *palmito* were consuming approximately 100,000 trees each month. Most of the wealth from production was exported from Guaraqueçaba, in fact exported from Brazil. The Caiçaras remained poor. By 1992, when *palmito* extraction was banned, the *juçara* industry was on the verge of extinguishing itself, and there was little opposition to the law. Today a few bootleg factories linger, conveniently overlooked by the local authorities. As outlaws, expecting at any moment to be closed down, these enterprises consume their resource like an inmate on death row eating his last meal.

Near the sea, the road to Guaraqueçaba gets a bit wild. Here the tropical forests transmute to mangroves. The word "mangrove" is an ecological term, not a taxonomic one, referring to various woody plants that are able to grow in shallow ocean water. Mangroves are a forest in the sea, at once terrestrial and marine. As salt water seeps into the coastal plain, conditions become hostile for most plants, and in the absence of competitors the mangroves take over. Equipped with a variety of mechanisms to expel salt from their tissues — ranging from exclusion to excretion to abscission of salty leaves — they have an adaptive advantage over all other woody plants. Few other species can survive here, and mangrove forests are therefore of low diversity. Only three species of mangroves — red, black, and white — eke out a living in southern Brazil. From the shore of the Baía de Laranjeiras, the red mangroves are the most conspicuous, striding through the water on arched prop roots several yards tall. Behind them, where conditions are a bit more terrestrial, are the black mangroves. Their roots, which would otherwise die in the anoxic mud, send up spiky snorkels that look like beds of nails. Farther back, in the driest zone, only occasionally reached by the spring tides, are the whites. Crossed by meandering channels and encompassing secret embayments, mangrove forests are confounding to navigate. The tide, however, slips through their legs easily, bringing the larvae of fish and invertebrates and motes of algae into an inverted, wet canopy. Many creatures are transients, spending only their juvenile stages in the mangroves and returning to sea as adults. Others are colonists and settle down. A single red mangrove prop root may be encrusted with a rainbow of red tunicates, yellow sponges, purple bryozoans, gray barnacles, black mussels, a few hardy corals (all or which have planktonic larvae), and pastures of pale green algae. Most animal species of the Baía de Laranjeiras and the sea beyond depend on the luxuriant mangroves as a nursery. The bay would die without them.

The still water among the mangrove roots is reddish-brown, like dilute tea. The color comes from tannic acid, the result of decomposition of leaves and wood. A great variety of plants, tropical and temperate, produce tannins, highly reactive compounds that bind with proteins and confound the internal workings of cells, as defenses against insects and other organisms. (Humans use tannins too: cutch, a tannin extract of mangrove wood, has been used to tan hides for centuries.) Mangroves, which are vulnerable to both leaf-eating insects and wood-burrowing marine worms, are especially rich in tannins. Paradoxically, mangrove forests are among the most productive ecosystems on earth, providing food for uncountable marine organisms down the food chain. Many larval fish and crustaceans, whose delicate guts are only a few cells thick, are able to feed on mangrove leaves without succumbing to the tannins. How do they do it? They feed on the mangroves only secondarily, through a pathway known as a detrital food chain. After the mangrove leaves have dropped into the sea, they are broken by the waves into smaller and smaller pieces. These detrital particles are rapidly colonized by marine

Arched prop roots of red mangroves striding across the water.

fungi, which have mechanisms to denature the tannins and which in their own right are highly nutritious. Eventually the pieces are only a few microns wide, just the right size to be eaten by larval fish and crabs, which digest only the edible coating; the rest, with its embedded toxins, passes intact through the animal's gut. After the particle is excreted, it may be colonized by fungus again — indeed, hundreds of times more — each time losing a modicum of its mass, until it is completely consumed.

Walking on the waterfront of Guaraqueçaba, I talk shop with João, a middle-aged Caiçara fisherman who is bailing his swaybacked sloop, the *Apollo 11*, in front of the fish market. *Apollo 11* is as crooked as the boards from which it was hewn, yet as hydrodynamic as a fish. High-prowed and high-sterned, it can take the assault of the waves from either end. I ask João whether he would be willing to take me into the Baía de Laranjeiras while he fished.

"Perhaps," he shrugged. "The fishing hasn't been very good recently. Will you buy us lunch?" He gestures to a boy folding the lanyards on the bowsprit.

"Is he your son?"

"Myself, I have eight living children, Senhor." João counts on his fingers: "Five boys and two girls."

At dawn the next morning, we slip from the village wharf over the quiet shallows of sea grass. The sail is furled in the still air, and João silently sculls from the stern with a rhythm exactly attuned to the sloop's rocking. For a while the surface of the bay is as smooth as glass. The water is flocculent with billowing green plankton and organic spume. Here and there the sediments have decanted, leaving the water transparent for at least a few yards. The sea in these light gaps scintillates with translucent fry, looking like slivers of glass. The bay bottom oozes with organic material. Mullet lunge from our path, leaving wakes of sediment and occasionally flipping entirely out of the water. Blue crabs, known locally as *siri*, oar over the sea grasses on flattened back legs as delicately as butterflies. When the boat passes overhead, they drop to the sea floor and raise their claws in anger.

All the lazy morning we scull past low-slung mangrove islands and mud flats that smell of sulfur and salt. The mangroves are draped with bearded *Usnea* lichens, giving them a disconsolate aspect. An American egret is hunting in the prop roots of a red mangrove, using the shade of the tree to help it peer into the water. Its reflection on the wrinkled bay is like a ragged white flag. The tide has withdrawn, and two great blue herons daintily pick at the exposed morsels on the mud flats, stepping with exquisite care among the black mangrove roots.

Following pages: A high-prowed Caiçara canoe on the Baía de Laranjeiras.

A fleet of brown boobies is in the sky ahead, investigating a blemish where pilchards rile the water surface. The birds dive head-first into the bay, then make long, splashy takeoffs that are clearly audible across a quarter mile of water. The pilchards scatter at the approach of our boat, etching the water like cracked ice. A pod of five spinner dolphins follows a nearby canoe, skillfully using it as a blind to capture fish. The fisherman, sitting on his oar, doesn't seem to care. Patience is his greatest skill. An osprey grabs a footful of water, drops its fish, then returns to the sky without getting wet. A white flotilla of ring-necked gulls bobs on the horizon where the ocean meets the bay. The same horizon is sewn by undulating lines of olivaceous cormorants; they disappear into the haze, then reappear, flying just above the surface of the water. Cormorants are like flying submarines. One suddenly bobs up next to the sloop, a fish in its bill. With great dexterity it repeatedly tosses and catches the fish until it is oriented head-first, then swallows it down.

Soon the waxing tide is working against us, and João lofts the sail. The boat has a mind of its own now. It shifts dramatically from one axis to the next, the boom unexpectedly crossing the deck. João doesn't know these passages, which change with every wind and rain, and we keep running aground in the mud. Weirs of stakes have been constructed across the tide, leading to corrals that trap migrating fish and crabs. As the morning clarifies, we see a mirage of white-sided boats anchored in front of the hardscrabble fishing village of Superaguí.

The village's most substantial building is the white stucco church. The houses have wattle-and-daub walls of African style, but their pastel-silled windows are European. Most of the houses are thatched; a few of the more prosperous ones have red tile roofs. Above one of the yards a flock of blue-cheeked parrots — as always, in pairs — is mobbing a gravid mango tree. From the boat, we can smell the village cooking fires. Every yard has a raised vegetable and herb garden, often in a broken, dirt-filled dugout canoe perched on stilts beyond the reach of the chickens and pigs. Every homestead has a usable canoe, too, heaped with yellow nets, tied to a stake on the mud beach. Among these islands, canoes are liberty. They are made in Pentaqueçaba — a nearby town of canoe artisans — of *guapiruvu* wood. Large *guapiruvus,* João tells me, grow deep in the Mata Atlântica and are getting rare now. The Caiçara canoes, which have keels to better manage the shifting tides and leaf-shaped oars to cut the running sea, are of the same design as those of their Tupinambá ancestors. The nets, however, are Portuguese.

At lunch we eat the sweet fruits of the sea in a makeshift bar in Vila Superaguí. Half the clients are big-spending day-trippers from the cities, who have journeyed here in powerboats.

An orange-winged parrot.

João contemplates them uneasily. The bar has a red tile roof and floor, painted pastel windows, stucco walls with murals of surreal fish, tables with blue plastic tablecloths. The shrimp are deep-fried and slightly pungent, and the lean fish are made fatty and satisfying with lard, oil, and batter.

Twenty million people live in the urban excrescence that is São Paulo, 140 miles from Guaraqueçaba. Two city blocks of São Paulo have more people than live in all of the Baía de Laranjeira, and that is the fundamental threat to the future of the region. The Caiçaras, relegated to an economic backwater, will always do what is expedient in the short term. Guaraqueçaba has been "discovered" as a quaint weekend playground. As in Ecuador, it is now a matter of triage, national decision-making about which surviving wild areas of the Mata Atlântica to save and which to sacrifice. The lowlands, decidedly agricultural, are already lost. But the Serra do Mar and its fringing mangroves harbor the largest remaining patch of the coastal forest. The decisions made during the next few years will determine whether this vicariant reflection of the Amazon forest will persevere and whether the great muddy nursery of the Baía de Larangeiros will continue to feed the sea and the people who live on its shore.

The Maya Mountains

The Human Signature

I CAN'T COUNT THE NUMBER of bird species I hear singing in the shaggy green mountains beyond the Macal River. I get to about fifteen and then lose track. The concert, which began as a solo — the descending flute of a dove in the cold, damp morning air with vestiges of fog clinging to the forest canopy — slowly evolved into a chorus as the warming sun crept higher. Now I hear tripping tanagers, mewing catbirds, staccato kingfishers, the *cow-cow-cow* of a violaceous trogon, and the tapping of a sapsucker on the flaking bark of a gumbo-limbo tree.

The forests of Cayo District, in western Belize, are low-growing and not diverse. The primary forests here disappeared several millennia ago; today we are left with the scraps. Strangely enough, recovering forests, full of light, are more productive than mature climax forests. They abound with nourishing seeds and insects that attract a characteristic suite of birds that is different from, and not as diverse as, those found in mature forests. Thus the morning's avian symphony. The forests of Cayo are dominated by a few conspicuous species: cohune palm, *copal, ramón* (breadnut), allspice trees, wild *sapote* (sapodilla), and bulletwood, which hog the nutrients and intercept the sunlight. Dominants like these are symptomatic of disturbance in tropical forests. Strangely, and hauntingly, the most common forest trees in Cayo District are the species that were once held in the greatest esteem by the classic Maya civilization. Every part of the cohune palm was used; the leaves provided thatch and the seeds cooking oil. *Copal* resin was burned as incense to repel evil spirits. The oily, starchy fruits of *ramón* were a staple of the Maya. Allspice berries yielded the same flavoring we use today. Wild sapote and bulletwood, both extremely durable, were used for construction. These were the economic species of an empire that for mysterious reasons collapsed about 1,200 years ago. Certainly the Maya must have enriched their forests with the trees they considered to have the greatest value. Can we still read this signature more than a millennium later? I think so. After all, twelve hundred years is only twelve generations of trees.

There is probably no such thing as a pristine forest in western Belize. Regardless, the mountains and valleys of Cayo District embody, for me, the mystery of ancient human presence and its passing. Near the village of Blackman Eddy, on the puny Western Highway, which runs from Belize City to Guatemala, are the ruins of Barton Ramie, a corridor of ruined pyramids 90 or a 100 feet high. At first they don't appear to be pyramids — steep hills, perhaps. But then you notice that some of the hills are flat-topped, truncated. The local people, mostly transplanted Africans, have built their houses right on top of the mounds. Do they know what's underneath? The extent of the ruins sinks in gradually, like a long daydream. These bedraggled villages and farms must have been a vigorous urban center at one time.

These temple facets, once painted orange and pastel, must have been the buildings of a great city, a religious center or emporium. The Western Highway, it seems, runs through the heart of this vanished metropolis.

The rocks and soils at Blackman Eddy are pale limestone. When the vegetation is removed, the land and monuments are tawny yellow. This is young earth, weathered from the floor of a sea that retreated tens of millions of years ago. The alkaline soils are self-liming, ideal for growing corn — and therefore ideal for growing civilizations. Domesticated corn coevolved with its human partners here. For more than four millennia these rich lowlands have been the breadbasket of the Maya.

The Maya ruins of Xunantunich, dating from the Classic Period.

When the Classic Maya civilization collapsed 1,200 years ago, the population of what is now Belize was approximately one million — four times what is today. The Maya had subdued the forests and fought wars in the valleys between these mountains. About 2,500 years ago they discovered lime cement and began to build their cities. By the Classic period, much of the population was living in urban centers such as Caracol, El Pilar, Xunantunich, and Cahal Pech, among others. The residents were royalty, merchants, administrators, soldiers, and, most important, engineer-priests. Like queen termites, these urban castes had to be fed by others, and the cities were dependent on agricultural products carried along trade routes from the surrounding forests.

According to some archaeologists, the priests were the keepers of secrets. Using a base-twenty mathematics, they calculated the trajectories of the planets and the apparent movement of the stars across the vault of heaven. They worked out the trigonometry of pyramids and converted forest to cropland. They imagined the void — the number zero — and its opposite, infinity. They contrived at least eight different glyphs for zero, in an effort to keep mathematics arcane and indecipherable by the masses. One of the glyphs for infinity was the wheel. Although the Maya used a wheel to divine the universe, they didn't use it for earthly transportation. They considered the circle too sacred to ever be enslaved as a tool. But their children's toys had wheels; they believed that children, in their innocence, could talk to the gods.

What ended the brief season of the Maya? Did the peasants rise against the theocracy? Did wars rend the fabric of civilization? Did the forest soils simply wear out? All of these scenarios are today being vigorously debated by scholars. Probably all three have elements of the truth. But the diminished forests of Cayo District strongly support the last scenario. Then, as today, fire was the Maya weapon that transformed Belize, Petén, and Yucatán to corn. How could the millions of maize-growers requisite to support the star-gazing theocracy not have bankrupted the soil and destroyed its diversity? Today the forests of Cayo are lacking whole groups of animals and plants that once flourished here. There are no monkeys, no macaws; only a few giant trees spread their century-old boughs over canopy and hill.

I wonder: What if this society had evolved on the steppes — much more forgiving of agriculture — and not in the tropical forest? Would it have sent ships across the oceans? Would base twenty be the norm in mathematics? From the Maya conflagration emerged the understanding of physics and math, the godly knowledge of astronomy. Must a culture immolate its home in order to grasp the ether, the invisible laws? The theocracy, when it died, took the knowledge with it. Today a smattering of land-bound, time-illiterate peasants and, worse, their indifferent Spanish conquerors, remain, poking through the ruined forest and the cinders of metropolis. For seven hundred years after the collapse, the Maya forgot the concept of zero; they had to relearn it from the Spanish.

A pyramid at the Maya ruins of La Milpa.

In the noonday sun, the steps of the temple are too hot to touch. This pyramid, and the approximately one hundred other monuments at Caracol, constitute one of the great archaeological discoveries of this century. During the Classic period, Caracol rivaled (and, at one point, may have conquered) the much more celebrated Maya city of Tikal. Caracol is a ghost town today, overgrown with trees of large diameter and high canopy. On this day in March, before the beginning of the rains, many of the trees are barren of leaves but flamboyant with flowers. The plazas are shaded by huge allspice, *ramón,* and *copal* trees, and the causeways are crowded with cohune palms. The oldest trees are burdened by pseudo-canopies, legions of reddish epiphytes and verdant green mosses that create tremendous, weighty burdens on their hosts' trunks. In this manner the epiphytes steal the light without having to invest in wood. They are, by any measure, parasites.

The Caracol pyramids are monuments to the maize- and *ramón*-growers' control of the reluctantly yielding earth. The temple is topped with a broad platform that catches all the hot, tossing winds from Petén. Today it is easy to climb to the top of the forested temples, using vines and saplings as hoists. The aristocrats and priests dwelled in chambers at the summits, descending to earth, it is thought, only for special events and ceremonies. The priestly chambers are shady, breezy, and cool. The walls are plaited with the insinuating roots of a strangler fig. The lintels over the doors, made of pale bulletwood and reddish sapote, are still intact — a bit moldy, perhaps, but strong. In many ways the people who lived on top of these pyramids were like epiphytes on the trees. The Maya believed that their gods came from the wind and the sky, and the priests and astronomers who resided in these aeries, conducting their arcane divinations, were the first to intercept the inspiration of the gods. Loft-dwellers, they were unable to mingle with the bottom of the food chain, lest their earthy appetites be perceived.

The terrain southwest of Cayo District is karst: eroded limestone mountains that have differentially dissolved, giving them the appearance of a frozen green, choppy sea. Some of the crests seem to be breaking in waves, like the "angry rocks" of traditional Chinese gardens. The karst country is the southern limit of limestone in central Belize. South of here are the Maya Mountains, intrusions of sandstone and quartzite named the Cockscomb and Mullins ranges, that have been revealed by the erosion of a plain of ocean-born carbonate sediments. The sandstone is an ancient sea floor, 250 to 300 million years old, twice as old as the sea whose limestone sediments sustained the Maya. The Maya Mountains are acidic, and their soils not conducive to agriculture. Never heavily populated, the mountains have stayed wild. During the days of the great urban centers of Tikal, El Pilar, and Caracol, the Maya disdained these mountains, which were the refuges of hermits and ascetics. Here were the miners who quarried the basalt for *metates*, the stone mortars and pestles for grinding corn that are the trophic symbol of civilization in Central America.

The Maya Mountains are an outlier of the vast, species-rich tropical forests of South and Central America, extending from the Amazon to Guatemala. They are the northernmost limit of several Neotropical groups, including trees in the genus *Virola* (red-sapped members of the nutmeg family), and the silver-and-turquoise-winged *Morpho* butterflies, which look like scraps of flying tinsel. Why have there been no cities here, ancient or modern? The reason is the so-called deceit of tropical luxuriance. The change from karst, which sustains agriculture, to silicates makes all the difference. Although the forests are tall and extravagantly diverse, they are poor in essential nutrients, such as phosphorus, potassium, and calcium. Most species-rich tropical forests, as in Amazonia, grow in impoverished, acidic soils. The shortage of nutrients means that no single species or suite of species can become dominant, pushing others to extinction.

A Morpho butterfly.

The northern spine of the Maya Mountains is the Cockscomb Range, the crown of which, Victoria Peak (3,675 feet above sea level), is the highest spot in Belize. Perhaps because they are devoid of human history and because their tops are almost always in the clouds, the Maya Mountains have remained surrounded by lore and confusion. In 1888 Governor Goldsworthy made the first ascent of Victoria Peak. The expedition, which departed from the coastal village of Stann Creek, took twelve days. Goldsworthy wrote, "This mountain and hill district we had explored, although so near to the coast, had never been visited and had always been enveloped in a cloud of mystery. . . . The native imagination had peopled it with evil genii and all kinds of mysterious creatures and the main peak was said to be surrounded by a lake and unapproachable by man."

The Sittee River, which drains the northern Maya Mountains.

THE MAYA MOUNTAINS: THE HUMAN SIGNATURE

The only recent occupation of the Maya Mountains has been by loggers, whose presence was inevitably transient. The first attempts at logging the mountains were made in the 1700s, and the industry continued sporadically until late in this century. Mahogany was the prize. Logs of the soft wood were hauled by oxen over steep mountain trails to the rivers, bound onto rafts, and floated to the coast, from where they were pulled by tugboat to Belize City. The loggers were a hardscrabble lot, isolated in an unproductive land. Typical of these logging camps was Quan Bank, which in the 1950s, at the peak of its activity, had sixty families, a sawmill, and an airstrip. The families, considering themselves transients, learned to harvest only a few products from the forest: the starchy rhizome of *comotillo*, a cycad, which was used as a *metate* ration in the absence of corn, and chicle, the white sap of the sapodilla tree, used to manufacture chewing gum. The loggers hunted white-lipped and collared peccaries and even killed and skinned the occasional jaguar. They were plagued by insect-carried diseases: malaria, yellow fever, and leishmaniasis, which was so common in the camps that it became known as "chiclero's disease." Food and other staples had to be imported, inevitably at inflated prices. Seldom did the loggers offer legal tender; the usual payment was in raw materials, the so-called bay currency: chicle, rubber, and mahogany. (Belizean rubber was extracted from trees in the genus *Castilla*, which is only distantly related to the Amazon rubber tree, *Hevea brasiliensis*, which has become the species of commerce over most of the world.)

In 1961, Hurricane Hattie flattened the forest around Quan Bank. By then most of the big mahoganies had been felled, and the difficulty of extracting the remaining legs over the washed-out trails and roads was becoming insurmountable. The last loggers left the Maya Mountains in 1989.

I am spending the afternoon hiking on the abandoned logging road that used to lead to Quan Bank. Here and there I can perceive the shelves cut by the hooves of the oxen that once dragged logs down this trail. The road, rambling west through a steep-sided valley, provides the only access to the Maya Mountains, at least for vehicles, from the Caribbean side. It is also the only gateway to Belize's celebrated jaguar reserve, home of an estimated twenty-five to thirty jaguars, more than live anywhere else in the country. The abundance of such a top predator says a lot about the vigor of the lower rungs of this ecosystem. Each jaguar, which may weigh as much as 250 pounds and be eight feet long, requires enormous resources: fourteen to fifteen square miles of undisturbed tropical forest replete with healthy populations of tapirs, peccaries, and other prey. Never having faced much competition from humans, the jaguars have prospered here.

The jaguar reserve is also one of the last stands of howler monkeys, known as "baboons" in Belize. Once howlers were common here, but their numbers were slowly diminished by the loggers, who relished monkey meat and found them, always conspicuously defending their territories, easy to shoot. But the loggers brought something far more pernicious than the rifle; yellow fever decimated the howler troops in the 1950s. Finally, in 1961, the relicts were driven to extinction by Hurricane Hattie. For thirty-two years the forests of the Maya Mountains were howler-silent, which is the auditory equivalent of felling a sequoia. You never forget your first encounter with the bellicose territorial blusterings of howler monkeys. Listeners have described them as sounding like a collective of demons or like anchor chains being dropped from an empty tanker. In May 1992 three lonely groups of howlers, totaling fourteen animals, were introduced from other parts of Belize into the area around Quan Bank.

There are no howlers singing this afternoon; sleepy in the heat, they will wait until dusk. But the dry-weather cicadas are shrilling from the canopy. The locals believe they are signaling that tomorrow will be a hot day. The closed forest is sewn by the undulating aromas of flowering orchids, which act like fishing lines to lure bees. Like all mature forests, it is a mosaic of light and shade. Cohune palms grow in sunny association with *Cecropias* in the light gaps. Many species in the understory spend their day waiting hopefully for a fleck of light, which lasts only a few minutes before moving on but provides enough energy for survival.

At the end of a long riverside trail among the tree ferns, where the granite has submitted to the river, is a waterfall. In its vicinity the temperature drops precipitously. *Morpho* butterflies and damselflies, which look like neon needles, rest in this misty shade, safe from the caustic sun. Nearby a column of leaf-cutter ants has cut a trail in the clay, hefting their burdens like parasols into their huge earthen mound. Leaf cutters can strip a tree in a matter of hours, leaving it blind to the nourishing sunlight. They do not eat the leaves, instead using them as mulch in their subterranean chambers and eating the fungi that they grow on this green paste.

In 1989, when the jaguar reserve was established, ten families of Mopan Maya — about seventy people — lived there. The forest probably couldn't have supported many more. When visitors started coming to the reserve, the ten families moved out of the forest, lured by the promise of earnings from tourism. They now run a roadside stand, selling sodas, crafts, and miniature *metates*. The Mopan Maya have entered the monetary economy of Belize with all of its risks and

A jaguar, the largest cat of the Americas.

pleasures. In a generation, they have journeyed from the forest to the middle class. The jaguar reserve is part of a larger, integrated conservation area that descends from the top of Victoria Peak to the bottom of the sea at the Snake Cays, at the landward edge of the Belize Barrier Reef. Three hundred miles long and between thirty and seventy miles wide, the barrier reef is the largest biological formation in the Caribbean, consisting of three atolls and innumerable smaller formations. It is second in size only to the Great Barrier Reef of Australia's Coral Sea. The descent from the Maya Mountains to the reef traverses one of the great panoplies of diversity in all of tropical America. The plan for the conservation area, designed by the Belize Audubon Society, embraces the concept of integrated ecosystem management that was pioneered by the Nature Conservancy. The planners understood that the survival of the offshore reef depends on the continuing health of the watershed that drains into the sea.

The shoreline east of the Maya Mountains is storm-pounded. It is the catastrophes — the infrequent hurricanes — that are the limiting factors here, periodically resetting the clock of ecological succession. Nothing, be it a tropical forest tree or a filigreed coral, can grow to full stature here. Yet these storm-battered conditions beget diversity, just as a tropical forest with a variety of regenerating light gaps packs in the most species.

North Stann Creek, the Sittee River, the Bladen Branch River, the Río Grande, and the Moho River all flow from the Maya Mountains to this ragged coast. The rivers flow through extensive banana plantations, where they pick up pesticides. Bananas, which are as soft and irresistible to insects as they are to humans, must be bombarded with toxins to survive in this tropical climate and still be the unblemished fruit that North American consumers demand. The rivers are wilder elsewhere: clear, cold, and shallow, overhung with forest. During the dry season a few sandy islands, shaped like tears, appear in their centers. During the rainy season it's a different story. The rivers, swollen and turbid, exceed their banks. Entire forests, it seems, slide into the sea, and the river deltas excrete plumes of silt that extend for miles. Eventually the mangroves that crowd the coast still the river water and decant much of the sediment.

*

Río Frío Cave, Mountain Pine Ridge.

The entire barrier reef was built by coral polyps and calcareous algae, animals and plants no larger than a thumbnail. Although corals are predatory animals, they also function as photosynthetic green plants by virtue of the mutualistic single-celled algae, known as zooxanthellae, that live in their tissues and that are, in part, the source of the corals' pastel colors. The zooxanthellae incorporate respired carbon dioxide and nitrogenous waste products created by the coral into their photosynthetic and protein-making factories; the corals breathe the oxygen and consume the carbohydrates produced by the zooxanthellae. It's a tidy and highly economical system. Functioning as both plants and animals, the corals have the best of both kingdoms. They are ravenous green rocks. And, like the trees of a tropical forest, the reef-building corals are engaged in a competition for real estate in the sun. There is a coralline imperative to evert, to spread skeleton and body surface over the earth, coating the rocks and neighboring corals with light-hungry flesh. As in the tropical forest, shade is lethal here. A coral will suffocate in the offending shadow of a towering neighbor.

Too much sediment is also lethal. Every coral polyp in this vast biome excretes a layer of mucus, which keeps the polyp clean by sweeping away sediments and debris. The mucus also intercepts the plankton captured and immobilized by its stinging tentacles and pushed by cilia toward the central mouth. Sand grains, passing in and out of the guts of urchins and sea cucumbers, mouthed by fish, are coated with secondhand mucus. Even the burrows of the sand-dwelling *Arenicola* worms, stacked just beyond the angle of repose, are coated with mucus; without it the burrow walls would collapse. A healthy reef, therefore, is coated with mucus; the bottom of the Belize Barrier Reef is a moving layer of slime. To mucus-loving bacteria and cyanobacteria, the interstices of these sand grains are a food-rich environment that extends for millions of square miles.

On a stormy afternoon in July, I go scuba diving on the Snake Cays, just offshore from the mouth of the Monkey River. The surge reverberates over the shallow isthmus between the cays, creating roving nodes where the waves intercept each other. On one of the cays is a stranded dugout canoe with no occupant.

These are the first days of the rainy season, and I can't see the windward forests of the Maya Mountains, obscured by clouds of their own making. Today the Monkey River is swollen with the angry new water, which brings more sediment than can be absorbed by the mangrove forests at the river delta. The milky water spills leaves, pieces of wood, and doomed seeds from the forest into the sea. The storm is stirring up the sea floor; visibility underwater is only a few yards. The shoals of sea grass rock like hysterical hula dancers in the surge. Insufficiently weighted, I am having a hard time keeping my equilibrium. There's plenty of organic ooze here to support the planktonic food chains on which the filter-feeding animals depend — so much, in fact, that the silt can strangle them; they can suffocate on their food. Only a few mucousy brain corals and gorgonians survive here. Some of the brain corals appear as if they had male pattern baldness, their tops killed by the sediment and infected with black line disease, an ecosystem in its own right, consisting of fungi and bacteria.

The Snake Cays are by any measure marginal. Farther offshore are the much more stable and therefore profuse reefs, the ones that attract tourists by the thousands to Belize. But the Snake Cays tell us more about the uneasy union of land and sea. Without the nutrients from the eroding land, this sea will starve. If there is too much erosion, it will smother. And it is here that the relationship will break down first. The Snake Cays are like a miner's canary, a place we should watch for danger signs. Their survival depends on the health of a forested range that neither the Maya nor the modern Belizeans ever wanted to settle.

An outpost of red mangroves in the shallow sea.

Río Lagartos

The Ragged Edge of the Continent

THE FLAMINGOS honk like treble geese, hidden in the salina behind the barrier island of Río Lagartos (River of Lizards, though *lagarto* often connotes crocodile as well. On some maps the estuary appears as Ría Lagartos, the Estuary of Lizards). The night wind smells of their guano. The moon, somewhere over Cuba, has not yet risen, but lightens the nimbus horizon. There are a few hard stars. A frigate bird, sleeping on the wing, floats silently in the void and now and again occludes a star.

Our dinghy drifts silently past a clump of mangroves. I stand in its prow, holding a spotlight against my forehead, scanning the dark water with its clarifying beam. And then, when the angles of incidence and reflection are exactly zero, I detect the reflection of a crocodile's eye, like a glowing ember in the night. The croc seems to be drifting in tandem with us. I bark at it, mimicking the universal crocodilian territorial call — a guttural *ungkh! ungkh!* — and it confidently turns toward us, gently oaring with its serrated tail. When facing forward, crocodiles have stereoscopic vision, and its eyes seem to make four reflections on the still water. It doesn't reply.

Crocodilian eyes at night.

Romeo, the boatman, doesn't know about this flashlight technique — a surprising innocence in Río Lagartos, where crocodiles have been hunted in this manner for generations. He sculls the boat as silently as an owl flying. Suddenly I lose my footing and kick an oar. The croc slaps the water with its tail and sounds. Still visible in the flashlight beam, it pushes a flower of silt and a shock wave of mullets over the floor of the lagoon. Occasionally the path of the light crosses one of the fish's eyes, which reflects turquoise. Confused, a mullet jumps into the boat, tearing its skin and splashing silver scales on the hard wood.

Ahead a nightjar, light-struck and still, is perched on the aerial prop root of a red mangrove. I am able to perceive each of the feathered vibrissae that fringe its bill. It blinks. Behind, I shine on the single, steady red eye of a snake. It, too, has binary vision, an adaptation for grabbing birds in the three-dimensional scaffold. The snake lounges like a vine in the dark boughs, from which sea-grass blades, bleached white in the wind, hang like tinsel.

The dry yellow scrubland of the northern Yucatán peninsula meets the sea at Río Lagartos, a crooked lagoon isolated from the Caribbean by a narrow barrier island. The Maya never constructed permanent settlements on the island. They knew better. At its northern limit, the peninsula, so verdant in Petén and Belize, loses its moisture and diversity. It's a pale terrain of calcium carbonate rock, low stone fences, a burning hot stubble of cornfields and tangles of jumbey bean. The locals, a mixture of Maya and Hispanic, call it the *tierra de faisán* (land of the great currasaw). The land is without nutrients. Some blame the depredations of henequen, the spike-leafed relative of the lilies that is made into rope and tequila, but the damage is much older.

This northern outpost of the Maya civilization has experienced 3,500 years of cultivation and empire, and when the Spanish arrived in the early 1500s, there wasn't much left. The surviving *hidalgos* of the conquest were awarded land on which they established rambling haciendas of henequen and cotton. Mission churches, sculpted from the local yellow rock, were built in every village. The churches are still the tallest features on the landscape. From their spires, one can always see the steeples in the neighboring villages: an early warning system against peasant uprisings.

Henequen, a thick-leafed succulent, and therefore well adapted to this arid land, served the local economy well, although it turned much of the land into a monoculture. But since the Second World War, rope has been made increasingly of inexpensive plastics, and the economy of fiber-producing areas has declined. Today the haciendas have been abandoned and the churchyards are overgrown with night-blooming moon cactus, which has vanilla-scented flowers a foot across.

Along this coast, the summer winds are easterly and the winter winds northerly; both are sea winds. The winter brings frequent storms, known as *nortes,* which cause the fishing boats to hie back to the safety of the lagoon. The summer brings hurricanes, which erase islands, build new ones, wind-sculpt the vegetation, and defoliate the spindly coconut palms. They set the clock of regeneration back to zero. On September 14, 1988, Gilbert,

A bed of nails: the pneumatophores of black mangroves.

one of the worst hurricanes of the century, demolished this coast; five years later, one can still read the signs of its passage: tree trunks splayed on the earth like the columns of a fallen temple, a broken-crowned canopy, and uniform cohorts of regenerating seedlings and shrubs.

From the mainland, the barrier island presents a horizon of green mangroves, silver lagoon, and sky. The mangroves are all striated northeast to southwest in general conformity to the easterly currents that bring drift seeds and flotsam from Cuba. The barrier is insubstantial and dynamic: one or two Pleistocene dunes, nudged from the sea, sparsely covered with thatch palms, Sargent's palms, and sea grape. Its far side, not visible from the mainland, is an empty white beach. Until the early part of this century, Caribbean monk seals hauled out on its shore. Unaccustomed to terrestrial predators, they were easy pickings for local hunters, who called them *lobos del mar* (wolves of the sea) and clubbed them to death where they lay. The last monk seal was seen on Seranilla Bank, a hundred miles east of Río Lagartos, in 1958. Today only a few old-timers remember them, and young people haven't a clue that such a large and conspicuous animal ever could have existed here.

The sand is mixed with crushed shells and brown algae. At the first spring tide millions of horseshoe crabs crawl onto the beach and, pushing themselves onto the sand with their clubbed back feet, lay their eggs. Seafaring reptiles also nest here. Female American crocodiles heap their eggs with mounds of vegetation beyond the reach of the highest tide and for most of the summer keep vigil. Moistened by the summer rains, the mounds slowly decompose; the heat of their decay incubates the eggs.

The first nesting female hawksbills, green turtles, loggerheads, and (rarely these days) leatherbacks arrive at the end of April and linger offshore until August, stealing onto the beach by night to bury their eggs. They probably hatched on this same beach decades before, for they can detect their natal shore by chemical cues. Since that time they have been at sea. The males will never return to the land, and the females will do so only during egg laying. They excavate shallow pits in the sand with their hind flippers, deposit their eggs, bury them, and retreat to the sea. By the following morning only the tracings in the sand reveal their passage. The local people can read these signs and raid the nests, harvesting the eggs, which look like Ping-Pong balls, and surreptitiously selling them in the nearby villages, where they are considered a male aphrodisiac. It is a mythical property, but the prospect of enhanced desire feeds an insatiable market that resists both common sense and law.

*

Río Lagartos is located on the fractured eastern rim of Chichxulub Crater, a great pock in the earth's face between 110 and 180 miles in diameter. Today the crater is filled with ocean, mangroves, and forest. From the earth's surface it is nearly impossible to discern the full dimension of Chichxulub. Satellite-borne radar provides the only accurate perspective. Formed approximately sixty-five million years ago, perhaps as the result of an asteroid or comet crashing into the earth, Chichxulub may be the scar of one of the greatest calamities to have befallen life on earth during its 3.5-billion-year history. Several square miles of calcium carbonate rock were instantly vaporized by the impact, which returned vast amounts of carbon, sequestered for millions of years in the shells of marine animals, to the atmosphere. The resulting cloud caused a pulse of carbonic acid rain that destroyed vegetation over much of North and Central America. Life for hundreds of miles around was erased. More important, the dust cloud and smoke resulting from the collision may have occluded the sunlight for several years, killing photosynthetic plants and the organisms that directly or indirectly feed on them. Plants with large seeds, or those adapted to long dormant periods in the soil, eventually regenerated. But in the meantime, the demolition of the food chains may have caused the demise of the dinosaurs, and in the darkened shallow sea the ammonites, shelled cephalopods that had been around for about 400 million years, also became extinct. In an instant, the trajectory of earthly evolution was forever changed. Vast new niches were opened up for the survivors, including the ancestors of the Río Lagartos crocodiles and the humans who shine them at night.

Today, driving across a scrubland whose memory extends only to the last hurricane, I find it impossible to imagine an event of such magnitude, caused by the indifferent and mechanical universe, or its role in the evolution of my home planet. The earth seems to have healed completely, although it is diminished by entire classes of animals and plants. Every year, hundreds of thousands of tourists are bused to the Maya ruins that are built in part from the fractured pieces of Chichxulub Crater. In awe of the Johnny-come-lately human civilization and the mystery of its vanishing, they are indifferent to the milestone of earth's history that took place here and that may have given their ancestors the chance to be.

The village of San Felipe is on the southern edge of Río Lagartos. Its white limestone streets are lined with crooked coconut palms and some drooping *Casuarinas*. The houses are made of sun-washed wood with pastel trim on their windows and doors. A few have corrugated tin roofs, glintingly hot on this afternoon, but most are thatched with palmetto leaves bound in fishnets, providing natural air conditioning. Almost all have a red-flowering geiger tree in the yard. The major obstacle is the stupefying heat, which makes every movement a toil and leaves one exhausted by midday. I am avoiding the heat by sipping a tepid beer in the waterfront disco. The floor is paved in cool blue tiles. A jukebox plays a Latino version of "Three Blind Mice."

Fishing dinghies, high-prowed, with blue and green trim, are tucked like sardines along the dock. They are made of modern composite material, not the gnarled native woods of the houses. Every one has a turnstone perched on its bow. Along the waterfront, the trunks of the coconut palms and telephone poles are painted in alternating red and white gesso. The poles are entire sapodilla logs imported from Petén, and unless a hurricane snaps them, they will last for centuries. Next to the limestone dock a flock of laughing women is drying conch meat, mending fishnets, and washing clothes. Paco and Lorenzo, two tame white pelicans, are waddling among the blowing laundry. A few of the children playing in the shade have sandy hair and startling blue eyes. Nobody knows why, but they are believed to be the descendants of the French pirates who once took refuge in the bays and lagoons of this coast. Jean Laffite is buried in a stucco-walled cemetery in Dzilám de Bravo, a few miles inland from San Felipe.

A traditional Yucatec house.

Most of the coastal settlements of northern Yucatán have sister villages, usually with the same name, fifteen to twenty miles inland, a phenomenon that considerably complicates reading maps. The villagers on the coast take refuge inland when the storms strike. The houses there are in the traditional Maya style: whitewashed mortared stone thatched with palmetto and twigs. The walls are curved, with no right angles. During hurricanes, oval houses are stronger than the square-jointed houses of European design. The inland villages may be safer than their coastal counterparts, but they are also prone to famine, for away from the sea there isn't as much to eat. A few permanent residents eke out a living raking backyard solar pans from which they harvest sea salt. Others work on the coconut palm plantations, but the market for copra is volatile, and many of the coconuts have succumbed to the most recent invader here, a mycoplasmal infection known as lethal yellowing.

*

Coconut palms beheaded by Hurricane Gilbert.

The northern coast of Yucatán lies along the shortest air route between Central America and North America and therefore is an important rest stop for migratory birds. Some species, such as the ruddy turnstone and the black-bellied plover, spend the winter here. Others merely bivouac. During the spring, swarms of migratory barn swallows fly straight east down the Río Lagartos lagoon. When they reach Cabo Catoche, at the northeastern tip of Yucatán, they head over the Gulf of Mexico to Cuba and then Florida. During the summer the resident shorebirds migrate between the interior and the coast according to the inland water supplies. Sometimes during the arid months of February and April, the mud-lined sinkholes known as *aguadas* desiccate, and the black-bellied plovers, golden plovers, yellowlegs, sandpipers, dowitchers, and whimbrels return to the shore. They return inland after the rains. At the end of the hurricane season in October, warblers and indigo buntings arrive from the United States in flocks of eight to twelve. The tiny birds have flown for twenty hours over the uncertain sea from the coasts of Texas and Mississippi and are desperately thirsty. The barrier island is as lethal as a desert, so they continue inland to the *aguadas*, which in good years accumulate a skin of fresh water. During dry years, when the *aguadas* are the only source of water for miles around, the migrants swarm like clouds of locusts.

Even in Maya times, Río Lagartos must have been a backwater. No civilization could have evolved on the arid northern coast of Yucatán. The moist volcanic soils that supported the Maya civilization are farther south in Guatemalan Petén and in Belize. There were Maya population centers a little south of here, associated with permanent bodies of fresh water known as *cenotes* and *peténes*. The *cenotes* are steep-sided sinkholes filled with fresh water. Connected to the sea through the porous Yucatec limestone, many are tidal, with a freshwater lens floating above salt water. The astronomical observatory of Chichén Itzá was built next to a *cenote,* which provided both drinking water and a place to fling the corpses of sacrificial victims. Today the bottom of that *cenote* is littered with human bones.

The *peténes* are larger bodies of water and are more diverse than the *cenotes*. Fringed by

shallow wetlands of lily pads and leather ferns and shaded by a canopy of sun-seeking trees 150 feet tall, the *peténes* are a different world where the sun doesn't enter. Even sounds are different: squeaking flocks of olive-throated Aztec parakeets, the tap of woodpeckers, the creaking of *Hyla* tree frogs, babbling ducks. The *peténes* are the last refuge of the Morlet's crocodile, which unlike its seafaring relative the American crocodile, is intolerant of salt water. Like its relative, the mother Morlet's crocodile builds a nest mound on the shoreline and guards it all summer long. The Morlet's crocodiles are trapped in the *peténes* with no option of escape, as veritably as the honeycreepers are trapped on Moloka'i. The *peténes* are their universe. Should the climate change and the *peténes* dry up, they would die.

*

The freshwater oasis of a petén.

Like all frontiers between the land and the sea, Río Lagartos is endowed with a splendid array of species and habitats: mangroves, sea-grass beds, high dunes on which grow a few salt-tolerant forest trees, and, where the shallow tide retreats over the muddy pink shallows, salinas. These pools of brine can be ten times as salty as sea water. They appear to be dead zones, ungraced by life. Salt crystallizes on the roots of mangroves and marches over shells and rocks; the water is a disturbing metallic pink. But their appearance is an illusion. Salinas are, in fact, a cellular soup of beta-carotene-rich bacteria and cyanobacteria, which thrive in these mineral waters to the exclusion of almost everything else.

The environment of the salinas is almost as old as life on earth, almost identical to the first simple ecosystems of the Archean Era, 3.5 billion years ago, when a young moon drew

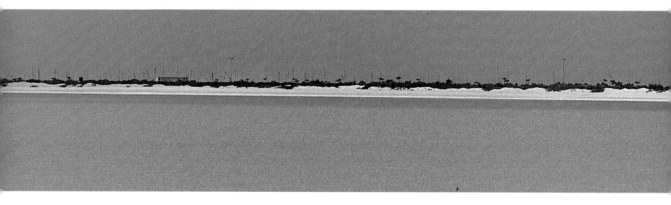

vast tides over the early continents and the most complex organism was a simple string of single cells. It has proved to be a successful and enduring ecosystem, although during the past 1.8 billion years or so, things have become a little bit more sophisticated: green algae now invade the salinas, creating laminated mats that pave the lagoon floor. Until the earth's continental shelves were dissected by ports and channels, a continuous biome of algal mats wrapped all the tropical and temperate land masses. The algal mats of Río Lagartos are typical of this vast biome. They are less than an inch thick, yet they have a canopy and an understory of different types of algae woven into a green scaffold. During the arid winter, the mats dry and crack, creating fractal shapes that seem to merge with the tracks of birds, resembling etchings by Escher. The mats curl and peel like old paint, then loft into the wind and disseminate for hundreds of miles.

During the spring and summer, rains fill the dry salinas, and the dissolved nutrients and implacable sun nurture an ephemeral eruption of life: brine shrimp, dark cyclones of midges, debilitating swarms of bloodsucking sandflies, nematodes, ostracods, copepods, mosquito fish, and the tiny, sharp-spired snail *Cerithium*. The air along the shallow margins of the salinas seems wormy and nearly opaque with black brine flies and mosquitoes dancing in the waves of heat.

Roseate spoonbills, olivaceous cormorants, and flamingos all converge on Río Lagartos to feed and reproduce. Since Maya times, the lagoon has been especially celebrated for its West Indian flamingos. Equipped with laminated, filtering bills, flamingos are the only large animals able to extract a living from the salinas. Heads inverted, they sieve brine shrimps and aquatic larval insects; they are especially fond of the *Cerithium* snails, which they swallow entire. The West Indian flamingo is a far-flung species that ranges from Aruba to Florida.

The salina at Río Lagartos.

In Yucatán, it occurs from the Bay of Campeche to Cozumel. Río Lagartos, in the middle of this range and remote from marauding raccoons and javelinas, is where they come to breed. Today the lagoon has the largest population of flamingos in Mexico: in 1988 there were approximately 20,000, a third of which were reproductive.

Flamingo sex is one of nature's great spectacles. During late March the adults and adolescents, restive, raucous, and hormone-charged, begin to congregate in the tidal flats and salinas. The males and females display to each other in abrupt salutes, flashing a wing and briefly revealing its startling black bar. The salina erupts in these staccato signals of black, one triggering the next until they cascade across the flock. By April, nuptial agreements, driven by instinct and pattern, have been sealed, and the pairs dance together in a formal waltz of stylized neck, leg, and wing movements. As more pairs form, the dance becomes communal. Legions of flamingos stride across the shallows neck to neck, pause, flash their wing bars, and then, like tango dancers, go into reverse. Robert Porter Allen, a naturalist who wrote the definitive book on the West Indian flamingo, described the spectacle as being "like a blazing prairie fire."

In April the mated pairs settle down to build their nests, which look like toy volcanoes about ten inches high, topped with a crater just as wide. They are made of the primordial stuff of the salina and are located in its scorching and inhospitable center, away from the mangroves and dune. Each pair lays a single egg, about twice the size of a chicken egg, which hatches in about a month. The mounds are designed to elevate the eggs above the muck, but in this capricious climate, they are often flooded, and the eggs and chicks of an entire season may be lost. In 1993 five hundred eggs were lost at Vayamíton, in central Río Lagartos, during a single sudden rain.

The drab gray chicks are short-legged and short-necked, the antithesis of the elegant, flamboyant adults. At first the demands they make on their parents are relatively heavy. For the first few days they feed on a blood-rich secretion of their parents' crops known as flamingo

milk, but as soon as they can walk they join crèches of other chicks. Both parents now are at liberty to feed and head off to other parts of northern Yucatán, but they return every few hours to feed their chick more milk. The parents are able to distinguish their chick from all the others in the crèche by the distinct timbre and pitch of its voice.

The chicks are weaned quickly and soon begin to sip the broth beneath their feet. Shedding their juvenile down, they acquire the plumage of adulthood and the ability to fly in about seventy-five days, and the beta carotene that laces their diet imbues the new feathers with their characteristic startling pink. Río Lagartos is a good place for the fledglings — safe from predation — and the juveniles spend the next two years there, eventually learning to migrate in chevrons above the breaking sea swells, where there are no obstacles (a broken leg means death to a flamingo), to other bays along the north coast. A favorite site is the Laguna Celestún, one hundred twenty miles west, whose mangrove-lined shallows are especially rich in algae and small animals.

West Indian flamingos.

The flamingos have an uneasy relationship with their human neighbors. Although flamingo meat has an overpowering odor of fish, it has traditionally provided an emergency food for people in a marginal land. The plump, flightless babies, which can be herded like sheep, are particularly easy prey. Robert Porter Allen described a flamingo hunt in the southern Bahamas in the early 1950s:

> The entire flock [of flamingos] piled up . . . in a confused and helplessly struggling mass. The raiding party, old women, boys, mongrel dogs and all, were upon them, arms and hands moving rapidly, feet kicking and crushing, canine teeth tearing and slashing. Slender necks and legs snapped like matchsticks. It was very little trouble. The brown bodies, with the bright promise of rose-pink beneath the newly developed wings, soon lay in heaps and in tangled mounds.

Today, the flamingos are protected in Yucatán, and the San Felipeños have entered the global economy. The biggest business, with 250 employees, is the salt company, established in 1947. It is a solar facility, borrowing energy from the sun and wind to evaporate embayed sea water in vast shallow pans, each several square miles in extent. Depending on the rains, the entire salt-creating process takes about eighteen months, as the water is shifted through a series of evaporating and crystallizing ponds, becoming progressively more saline. Each pond in the sequence yields a particular product. Sea water, which has a concentration of salts of approximately 35 parts per thousand (ppt) parts of water, bears a medley of dissolved compounds. At 60–120 ppt, sulfates and carbonates of calcium precipitate from the brine; at 120–200 ppt, the other sulfates; at 200–260 ppt, gypsum; and finally, at 260–270 ppt, several chloride salts, including commercially valuable sodium chloride (table salt). At this stage, only magnesium chloride remains, and it is flushed back into the sea.

The flamingos adapt easily to the salt pans, which are chemical and biological mimics of the salinas. At Río Lagartos, salt production is not only a physical but also a biological process: the flamingos, in fact, accelerate salt formation, because their feces inoculate the ponds with pigmented microbial flora that trap the sunlight and capture its heat. Other animals help too. Wind-blown brine shrimp, which can tolerate salinities up to 220 ppt and temperatures up to nearly 100 degrees F, also import the hypersaline bacteria that are necessary for the process of crystallization.

Mud cracked by the drying wind and sun.

Conscientiously managed salt pans make good flamingo habitat. There is no reason why solar salt facilities and flamingos cannot be exemplars of coexistence. Ultimately, however, the goals of the salt company are in conflict with the culture, land, and sea of Río Lagartos. When poor fishermen take the relatively high-paying jobs at the company, they abandon the sea and lose their knowledge of its ways.

The barrier island, barely emergent from the restive sea, is marginal and ephemeral. Winter steals the sand and the summer returns it, but the system is never quite in equilibrium. Hurricane Gilbert broke a channel 180 feet wide and 6 feet deep across the island, flooding the salt pans and turning the clock of crystallization back to zero. To save itself, the salt company repaired the island, closing the channel and consolidating the dune by bulldozing beach sand a few yards inland (which they continued during the sea turtle breeding season). These activities affronted the natural shifting of the sands. The salt pans — and for that matter the salinas — must be isolated from the open sea in order to function. Yet without the regular flow of sea water into the lagoon, the fish and invertebrates that use it as a nursery will die, the red mangroves will succeed to more terrestrial black and white mangroves, and the crocodiles, white ibis, and roseate spoonbills will flee. Migrating birds will change their patterns. Flowing sea water brings the breath of diversity to the lagoon of Río Lagartos, just as its absence, deep in the salinas behind the barrier island, creates a community that harks back to the beginning of time. As long as the barrier island emerges and disappears in the turning surf, there will be a mosaic of salinities and habitats at Río Lagartos. If the island becomes merely a dam, however, then the lagoon will become an Archean industrial wasteland.

The dike around a salt pan.

The Everglades

Sea of Grass

THE EVERGLADES has the aspect of a limitless seascape, as if a tranquil ocean had poured over the horizon and spilled onto the land. Driving the Tamiami Trail between Miami and Naples straight northwest across the Everglades, past Seminole and Mikasukee villages, alligator wrestling show towns and honky-tonk junk shops, teaches one the astonishing marginality of this place. A few yards above sea level, it is a mix of land and swamp. It is also a youthful landscape, where juggernaut hurricanes smash every few years. No tree lives to a ripe old age, and the oldest hummocks, rising like the smooth backs of turtles, are only thirty or forty feet high. Scattered over the wet plain, the hummocks provide neither scale nor perspective. From the levees of the Tamiami Trail, the encircling horizon absorbs the eye, and the water is as black and clarifying as a mirror, reflecting the billowing cumulus clouds that drift in from the Gulf of Mexico. Yet from the vantage point of a canoe, only three feet lower, there is no horizon. Instead there is a claustrophobic world of high sawgrass and cattails. Marjorie Stoneman Douglas aptly called these swamps the "River of Grass." On sunless summer days, only the seeping water, easing southwest, stilled here and there in a gator hole, reveals the ordinates of the compass. One navigates by watching the slight trajectories of green plankton.

The Everglades was once the bottom of a shallow sea paved with the calcium carbonate–rich shells of innumerable corals and calcareous algae. Long ago the sea retreated, but not by much. Now the Glades is the heart of a system of sheeting water that flows from the Kissimmee River through Lake Okeechobee to the Bay of Florida — a total of 22,000 square miles. (The only sheet flow of comparable size in North America is the shared delta of the Usumacinta and Grijalva rivers, in the Bay of Campeche in the Mexican state of Tabasco.) Nowhere is the water much more than three feet deep, and in most places it is less than a foot.

Lake Okeechobee, only sixteen feet above sea level, was a natural buffer, absorbing the summer flux from the Kissimmee and releasing it as a slow and deliberate seepage. Once the Kissimmee meandered articulately through the live-oak forests and savannas of north-central Florida, following the whim of contour and season. Today most of the Kissimmee has been straightened and canalized by heavy machinery, forced to conform to the mandates of agriculture. No longer do its floodplains embrace and still the summer rains.

The hummocks provide welcome respite from the unrelenting sun and water. Their centers are clones of bald cypresses; the founding trees are in the shady interior, with the juveniles tapering off toward the edge. The highest hummocks have emergent deciduous gumbo-limbo trees, whose orange boughs in winter look like swollen veins. Gumbo-limbos are able to regenerate from a splintered trunk or a fallen limb. Old-timers used to stick hewn

branches into the soil and grow them as living fences. They are immortal, at least on the temporal scale of the Everglades. Wax myrtles crowd the margins of the hummocks, vying for the last scraps of terra firma and light. During the summer the myrtles produce small berries, as hard and oily as beads of candle wax. I have watched a cloud of swallows, like a reverse cyclone, descend on the laden shrubs and in a few clamorous minutes strip them of their bounty. The swallows are stoking themselves with carbohydrates for their autumn migration to Cuba, Yucatán, and South America. You have to watch your step on the hummocks. Covered with mud, the limestone rag is razor sharp and will shred one's shoes and lacerate one's ankles. Jittery brown mangrove snakes and lethargic, venomous water moccasins, their black skins heat-absorbing, like to bask in the sunny dryness. Sometimes hundreds of snakes will congregate on a single hummock.

A buttonwood mangrove leaning over an ephemeral rainwater pond.

On Cretaceous summer evenings when the atmosphere seems liquid and every cold-blooded creature is too heat-antsy to sleep, the alligators boom over the swamp. Their guttural voices travel for miles just above the surface of the water, like thunder. During the summer, the mother alligators deposit their eggs in nests of warm, decomposing vegetation. Like the crocodiles of Río Lagartos, the mother alligators stay near their mounds and defend them. After approximately two months, the hatching baby alligators call to their mothers from inside the egg. The mothers scrape away the incubating vegetation and release the hatchlings from their natal bondage, gently clasping them in jaws big enough to dismember a feral pig and carrying them to the water.

Nothing is certain here, even the water, which today seems so pervasive. The weather brings either drought or torrents, according to the plan of El Niño; no year is quite like the previous one. In 1994 I walked among the hummocks on cracked mud as flat and firm as a parking lot. The fish and turtles had retreated to the depressions excavated by the large bull alligators. The gator holes, naturally rich in phosphorus from the bone-silted excrement of their makers, had become refuges, pockets of life in a place that had suddenly turned hostile. Life was easy for the alligators then. They simply picked off whatever food they needed. But in the summer of 1995 Florida is being buffeted by a trough of moist air from the Caribbean Sea, and the rains have returned with a vengeance. The dry hummocks have become refuges for feral pigs, raccoons, possums, white-tailed deer, and even the occasional panther. Unlike the gator holes, the islands are places of starvation. The deer trip from one hummock to the next, searching for browse. At first one sees only their white splashes, like a flat stone skipping across the water. Only later does one perceive the animals, earth- and water-toned, concealed by the colors of the flooded land.

Ultimately the problem is neither drought nor flood. It is the destruction of the natural modulators, of the earth's capacity to assimilate the shocks. The Everglades is now fringed by a rime of concrete urban sprawl and farmland. The waters, which once ran freely over the marl, are now enslaved, diverted through canals to the green lawns of Miami and to the flat expanses of sugar cane plantations south of Lake Okeechobee. The Tamiami Trail and Alligator Alley, both of which traverse the Everglades, are as unyielding as lines drawn on a map. They have become virtual dams. The sheeting water, once seemingly unlimited, has become a rare commodity, and people have started bickering over it.

Until the turn of the century the Everglades was considered an uninteresting outback.

In 1900 only about 30,000 people lived in all of Florida south of Lake Okeechobee, 18,000 of them in Key West. It was a place of wastrels and commercial plume hunters, who shot millions of egrets and storks to supply the trendy fashions of the north. The hunters especially sought the snowy egret, whose ivory plumes are as filigreed as a lace doily. Florida was beginning to urbanize, and the conventional wisdom of the time was that swamps were wastelands, barriers to progress. During his campaign for governor in 1904, Napoleon Bonaparte Broward promised "to drain the Everglades once and for all." Broward also started the conurbation that is now Miami, Fort Lauderdale, and West Palm Beach, constructed on the narrow strip of dunes and barrier islands between the Atlantic and the Everglades — an area intrinsically unsuited for urbanization. Since the 1920s, Florida has become a population sink for the overwrought cities of the North. Millions of retirees have settled into brand-new communities that are as uniform as Levittown: straight streets, bland green lawns, and golf courses. The cities are insatiably thirsty. Today more than 5 million residents, plus 39 million vacationing "snowbirds" per year, depend on the Everglades for their water supply.

Palmetto scrub.

Unappreciative of the local biological treasures, these urban refugees brought their own alien plants as ornamentals and as allies in a misguided war against the swamp: cajeput trees, Brazilian pepper, and *Casuarina*. During the 1930s cajeput, a eucalypt from tropical Queensland, was intentionally seeded by airplane over the Everglades. Cajeput is a land-builder, renowned for its high transpiration rate and therefore for its ability to drain the swamps in which it grows. It accomplished its mission. Today vast parts of the Everglades are monocultures of cajeput as uninspiring and as dry as a field of Iowa corn. The understory of a cajeput forest, dark as dusk and laced with the characteristic aromatic, toxic eucalypt oils, tolerates no diversity.

Brazilian pepper, a relative of poison ivy and poisonwood, bears ornamental red berries. Wintering robins find the berries irresistible and spread them in their feces. In South America, where it is native, Brazilian pepper is an aggressive colonizer of light gaps in the subtropical forest. From the perspective of a Brazilian pepper plant, most of southern Florida is a giant light gap. Today there is no roadside or other disturbed area without exuberant stretches of the shrub — hundreds of monotonous miles of the same species gone bonkers. And *Casuarina* trees, the so-called she-oaks or whispering pines of tropical

Australia, have choked the first dunes behind the sea, smothering them in fallen leaves as thin as pine needles. Most Floridians would declare that the wind-sighs of the *Casuarina* are one of the pleasures of living in the state, as Floridian as the alligator. Yet its leaves release toxins that make the soil unhospitable to competitors. They have converted the roadsides and beaches into a whispering monotony.

Starting in the 1940s, while the Atlantic dunes of Florida were becoming urban, the hardscrabble blacklands south of Lake Okeechobee were being converted to agriculture. Seven hundred thousand acres, amounting to about half of the greater Everglades ecosystem, were designated the Everglades Agricultural Area. The lake itself was imprisoned behind an earthen dike, and its effluent, which was once 150 miles wide, was constrained into canals. Several of the canals bled directly into the Atlantic without ever entering the sea of grass. Others fed the burgeoning sugar cane and vegetable plantations. The pace of canalization accelerated after the autumn of 1947, when two hurricanes battered southern Florida; the damage cost $59 million, a vast sum for the time. Although the true culprit was the uneasy proximity of the cities to the sea and its storm surges, the public response was to further contain the swamp-lands. From 1948 to 1971, the Army Corps of Engineers dug 1,400 miles of canals and installed innumerable locks, barriers, and electric water pumps across the original sloughs.

By 1994, 80 percent of the Everglades Agricultural Area, approximately 500,000 acres, was carpeted in sugar cane. The American appetite for sugar had become insatiable; each of us eats sixty-five pounds per year, and the Florida sugar harvest, estimated to be worth about $700 million, was about half of the total produced in the United States. Sugar cane requires the application of fertilizer that is rich in phosphorus, an element that used to be rare — and therefore limiting to the growth of plants — in the Everglades. Inevitably the water released from the agricultural zone into the Everglades was tainted with phosphorus, providing a surfeit of riches. The fertilized zones have become choked by phosphorus-demanding species such as cattails, which were once kept in check by the absence of the mineral. Today a great swath of dark green cattails, from Lake Okeechobee to Belle Glade, can be discerned by an orbiting satellite.

The environmental costs of the farms are obvious, but there are also social consequences. The sugar harvest depends on migrant labor, mostly immigrant Jamaicans and Haitians. Among the poorest people in Florida, they live in decrepit temporary barracks and are often alienated from public schools and government services. The low wages paid to these people are requisite to the labor-intensiveness of the crop; it takes about twenty-two person-hours of labor to harvest a ton of cane.

One would expect the Okeechobee sugar plantations to compete poorly in the world market. Because most of the world's sugar is produced in developing countries where labor costs are lower, sugar has become one of the most abundant and cheap products on earth. Rather than entering this international competition and saving American consumers millions of dollars, Florida's sugar industry has been protected by a complex and generous system of federal government quotas, resulting in prices that are well above world market levels.

Why has such an unviable economy been sustained? The answer is geopolitical. Ninety miles south of Florida is Cuba, the New World's largest supplier of sugar and until 1959 the largest exporter of sugar to this country, providing an estimated 3.2 million tons per year. In 1960 Fidel Castro nationalized American corporations in Cuba, seizing hundreds of millions of dollars in assets. President Eisenhower retaliated by imposing a debilitating trade embargo on the island. Seeking to ensure a steady domestic sugar supply, he offered economic incentives to sugar plantations in Florida, Puerto Rico, and Hawaii. The drained flatlands around Lake Okeechobee, yielding 36 tons of cane per acre (compared to 21 in the established plantations in Louisiana), were demonstrably suited to sugar production and therefore given highest priority. It was, by any measure, a sweet deal, but the Everglades, once the greatest wetland in the United States, succumbed to the Cold War.

The river of grass ends in the vast mangrove forests that fringe Florida Bay. There is true wilderness here. From the air, the meandering channels that separate the mangrove forests look like veins on a retina. The marly flatlands are encrusted with the same species of pink cyanobacteria and bacteria as the salinas of Río Lagartos, and the deeper bays and ponds are alarmingly green, like copper verdigris. Here, the cloud shadows look like hummocks. The ocean edge is a series of long, white beaches fronting pale, grassy swales. There is an occasional human mark: a straight and certain channel.

By the time the water has percolated through cattail and sawgrass, it is nearly bereft of nutrients. The prop roots of the mangroves ease the water from the Everglades into the bay, and as in Guaraqueçaba, they restore nutrients in the form of detrital particles. Until recently, Florida Bay was an estuary with a salubrious mix of salt and fresh water. Its average depth was only about six feet, so it was light-saturated and, during the summer, bath-water warm. The bay bottom, paved with billions of blades of sea grass, collected the sun's energy and transmitted it into the metabolism of a complex ecosystem of sponges, crustaceans, worms, and fish. As in Guaraqueçaba and Belize, the shaggy carpet of sea grasses, a foot high, immensely increased the surface area on which epibiotic plants and animals could grow. One survey counted sixty-four species of diminutive epibionts — including calcareous tube worms and corallike hydroids — that specialized in growing on turtle-grass blades. The bay was a nursery for the grass-hovering tarpon and bonefish and for the furtive snappers that lived among the mangrove roots. For nearly a hundred years it sustained a sponge industry run by the Greek community in Saint Petersburg.

A meadow of sea grasses, Florida Bay.

The health of Florida Bay depended on the breath of fresh water from the Everglades to compensate for the high rates of evaporation during the summer. When the canalization of the Everglades diverted this life-giving flow to the Atlantic, the bay acquired a burning salinity — several times that of sea water — and began to die. Florida Bay was becoming a huge salina. A salt-loving marine slime mold spread over parts of the sea floor. By 1995, more than 100,000 acres of sea-grass beds had died, and windrows of blades, as white as confetti, were piled high on the beaches. Their die-off created heaps of organic material that in turn fostered dramatic blooms of algae. Adapted to a cycle of boom and bust, the algae by day oxygenated the water and by night robbed it of dissolved oxygen. As oxygen levels declined, the sponges, which are animals that rely on the dissolved oxygen, blanched and died, looking like pale, drifting corpses. More than a hundred square miles of the bay's bottom, known as the dead zone, turned necrotic, generating bubbles of sulfide gas. One of the last great American wildernesses was dying.

The southern margin of Florida Bay is the archipelago of the Florida Keys. Washed by the Gulf Stream, a clear-water messenger from the Caribbean, the Keys and the shallows that surround them appear tie-dyed when seen from 30,000 feet, fractal swirls of turquoise and brown. The upper Keys are Pleistocene leftovers, littoral dunes of an ancient landmass that once included Florida Bay. They are highly permeable oolitic limestone saturated with sea water on top of which floats a lens of fresh water. The lower Keys, in contrast, were trussed up from Pleistocene sandbanks when the sea level was approximately 300 feet lower than it is today. The ancient winds stretched the sand northward like a plume of smoke. Extensive coral reefs lie on the south side of the Keys, in striated systems of spur and groove that range in depth from a few yards to the cerulean wall a mile deep at the edge of the Gulf Stream. The Gulf Stream is flecked with shaggy rafts of brown gulfweed or sargassum; a few, launched by eddies into the shallows, strand on the beaches in scratchy heaps.

Coral reefs grow only in waters warmer than 70 degrees F. The reefs of the Keys, at the northern limit of reef-building corals in the western Atlantic, assaulted by winter storms, cold fronts, and even the occasional snowstorm, are barely hanging on. The cold has stripped them of the most vulnerable species and they have only a fraction of the diversity of, for example, Belizean reefs. But as the only coral reefs in the continental United States, they are beloved, and a huge tourist industry is now devoted to them.

Recently, the caustically salty water of Florida Bay, leaking through the interstices of the Keys, has pushed the reefs to the brink. The first signs of distress, the so-called coral bleachings, appeared in the mid-1980s. The coral polyps began committing suicide, expelling their pigmented zooxanthellae. Unable to fix the sun's energy, the living skin of polyps slowly died and was replaced by a light-hungry community of shaggy brown algae. Everything else was imperiled as well. No longer did the scaffolds of elkhorn and staghorn coral vault into the light-rich sea, endowing the reef with uncountable secret places where a myriad species could make a living. The reef was becoming a bland platform of rock and algae.

*

Florida Bay: a mottled sea floor of sand and sea grasses.

The Florida Keys bear unexpected names that reveal their histories: First National Bank Key, No Name Key, Big Pine Key, Big Torch Key, Little Torch Key, Knockmedown Key and Little Knockmedown Key, Cudjoe Key, Sugarloaf Key, Saddlebush Key, Boca Chica Key. But these names are murmurs from times past, when the Keys were distinct from the rest of America. Today Highway I, the beleaguered road that threads the Keys, is pure honky-tonk: cheap motels, bars, rattan boutiques, palm readers, pawn shops, tattoo parlors, T-shirt outlets, and other sprawling ticky-tack. The road is lined with walls of red oleander, a poisonous but aromatic alien. During the tourist season the traffic rivals Manhattan's, both in magnitude and incivility. The jumbled roadside telephone poles seem to queue up as disobediently as the tourists at the Dairy Queens.

A few pieces of wilderness still remain. Large parts of Key Largo are still forested in hardwoods. Like the coral reefs, these forests, mostly of Cuban and Bahamian origin, are outposts at the limit of their ranges. And like the coral reefs, they may not survive much longer. Lacerated by Highway I, the Key Largo forests are being carved into retirement meccas. The real treasures of this archipelago — and the places that are most likely to endure — are the small forested keys only a few acres in size. One of these refuges is Lignumvitae Key, a 280-acre islet about two miles north of Matecumbe Key. Lignumvitae Key was privately owned — and nurtured — for more than half a century. But in the mid-1960s it was purchased by a group of Miami investors who planned to convert it to an upscale vacation retreat, making it homogeneous with the rest of the neoplastic sprawl along Highway I. The project would have been the *coup de grâce* to one of the last mature stands of West Indian forest.

There is no place quite like Lignumvitae Key. Covered by a mixed forest of 30-foot-high trees, it supports the largest mahogany trees growing in the United States, as well as gumbo-limbo, poisonwood, pigeon plum, mastic, darling plum, Jamaican dogwood, and strongback — in all, sixty-five species of woody plants. During the spring and autumn, these forests are a favorite bivouac for migrating warblers, vireos, and even the occasional Bahama bananaquit, which eats the hordes of insects that fatten in the forest during the spring and summer rains. Most unusual for an island so recently emerged from the ever-changing sea, the key supports one endemic species: a pastel-striped tree snail in the genus *Ligula,* which plasters itself to the trunks of mastic and mahogany trees. Animals of low mobility that cannot survive immersion in salt water, *Ligula* had speciated or subspeciated throughout the Keys since the end of the Pleistocene. Once each island had its own variety, but by the 1960s, most species had become extinct due to deforestation.

A Ligula *tree snail.*

A rare survivor: a 300-year-old lignumvitae tree.

Lignumvitae Key has been saved. In 1967 it was purchased for $2 million with funds from the Nature Conservancy and the National Audubon Society and presented to Florida as a state botanical site. Ironically, the price was inflated by a bidding war that included conservationists. Today the key survives, a Pleistocene leftover and a time capsule of Old Florida, little changed since the Spanish conquest.

The Spanish, seeking El Dorado and the Fountain of Youth, were the first Europeans to see Florida. In 1515 they began trading in the Keys with the Calusa Indians, a marine culture that constructed artificial islands, causeways, and kitchen middens of millions of whelk and oyster shells around the perimeter of Florida Bay. The trade was in the peculiar products of the Keys. The Calusas caught songbirds — mostly mockingbirds and cardinals — by coating branches with the sticky resin of gumbo-limbo, and exported them to the tobacco mills of Cuba, where the birds' songs broke the monotony of rolling cigars. Strongback, widely regarded as a male aphrodisiac that endowed men with the requisite "strong back" for prowess in lovemaking, was also an item of commerce during the Spanish occupation. The pounded bark of Jamaican dogwood was sold as a fish poison. Mahogany, which yields the soft, russet wood so prized for cabinetmaking and furniture, was sawed in place and shipped as far away as Spain. By the 1700s, commerce had nearly extirpated the mahogany; even now, there are almost no mature trees on the islands.

But the most celebrated export was lignumvitae, the wood of the gnarled tree that gave the key its name. It is a relatively small, slow-growing tree, seldom exceeding 30 feet in height, with wood so dense that it sinks in water, is difficult to saw, and is almost impossible to shape. But once fashioned into an object, lignumvitae is nearly indestructible; moreover, it is self-lubricating. The sugar mills in Haiti and Cuba turned on rollers and bearings made of lignumvitae, and therefore so did much of the economy of the New World.

But these qualities paled compared to another property — probably apocryphal — of lignumvitae, which made it as valuable as gold during the first decades after the Spanish arrival. In 1493, Christopher Columbus returned to Spain with a disappointing trove of gold and riches and no clue as to the location of the Fountain of Youth. History remembers instead that Columbus's crew brought home a New World pestilence: syphilis. (Whether syphilis — perhaps masquerading as its close relative, yaws — was already in Europe in 1493 is a question of considerable debate. Clearly, however, a new and virulent strain was introduced to Spain after Columbus's first voyage.) The disease spread rapidly across Europe in the ensuing decades. At first it was a killer, but over the decades it gradually lost its virulence, until by the early 1600s it had become the chronic, debilitating malady that we know today.

The early treatment — mercury — was as bad as the scourge itself, and the symptoms of mercury poisoning — drooling and dementia — were often incorrectly attributed to the disease. Mercury compounds remained the only effective treatment until the invention of penicillin in this century. But there were many ersatz remedies, each of which had a brief period of celebrity. One was a decoction of lignumvitae bark, which the tribes of the West Indies claimed cured the disease they had bestowed on their conquerors. As syphilis spread across Europe, so did lignumvitae. Only the rich could afford fresh bark from which to make their teas. The middle class extracted what they could from the leavings of the rich man's brew, and the destitute were allowed, for a few farthings, to worship pieces of lignumvitae that were hung from the altars of churches. Lignumvitae has never been proven effective, so worship was probably as effective as the tea itself.

All these commercially important plants are still found in Lignumvitae Key, making it a historic as well as a biological treasure. On this June afternoon, at the beginning of the summer rains, the deciduous gumbo-limbos are unfolding pale green leaves, the *Ligula* snails are plastered to the trees like miniature Christmas ornaments, and the cicadas are deafening. A Shaus's swallowtail butterfly sips white sap oozing from a wounded strangler fig. Two white-crowned pigeons, their crops distended like goiters, are gorging on the abundant green-black fruits of poisonwood, indifferent to their toxin. These birds are relics of an immense population that ranged from Florida to the Virgin Islands; the white-crowned pigeon was to the West Indies what the passenger pigeon was to the temperate United States. While sailing not far from here in the southern Bahamas, Columbus described them in vast "squadrons . . . that obscure[d] the sun" and that stretched as far as the eye could see.

Like the subtropical forest of Mbaracayú or Ecuador's tropical *ceja de la montaña*, Lignumvitae Key needs a mixture of light and shade to encourage and maintain a diverse mix of understory and canopy species. But today the forests of the key are tangled and dense. The last major hurricane was Donna, in 1960. Conditions have been stable too long, and constancy has diminished the biological diversity here. Now Lignumvitae Key needs another hurricane to open its forest canopy. It is waiting for the inevitable.

Following pages: A regenerating gumbo-limbo tree, tipped over by a hurricane.

When the big storm arrives, its accompanying tidal surge will also redraw the contours of the Keys and change the courses of channels. For a while, the Everglades will be awash and Florida Bay will be flushed clean. Islands will disappear and emerge and hummocks will be pushed back into the marl. The ramshackle shanties will blow away. The waves will liberate vast stores of sequestered mangrove detrital particles as well as long-abandoned pesticides, such as DDT, from the sediments. Some places will be poisoned; others will be renewed. The world will turn over, and this marginal land will begin anew.

An algal mat among black mangroves, Big Pine Key.

The Flying D Ranch

Resurrection

THE PRAIRIE VALLEYS of eastern Montana are brand-new ecosystems, sculpted by the retreating glaciers only 12,000 years ago. They haven't had time to age and mature, to evolve a bouquet of woody diversity. It is a landscape of absence, with no reliable supply of water. The only lakes are artificial wallows for cattle; most are hoared by excrescences of salt. A junk car lot, glinting with metal and glass, also resembles a mineral exudate. Wheat fields, plastered to the ridge tops and following the amorphous vagaries of irrigation, are like tan Panamanian *molas.* The rivers are shallow and braided with alluvium, and during particularly dry years they disappear entirely; the powdery arroyos are susceptible to flash floods. Forests crowd the arroyos, which after a fresh light snow look like dendrites of frost on a winter window. Most of the trees are stunted by the dryness and cold winter winds. A century-old tree is a rarity here, and an outcropping of trees on the stark plain is as simple and startling as a Japanese Zen garden.

This is cowboy country. Like Antisana and Guaraqueçaba, it is a land that has been changed by cattle ranching, an activity for which Americans have a great nostalgia, but one that robs the land of its true personality. There is little of what Lewis and Clark found here 190 years ago. Cattle, the foundation of the local economy, have reworked the mantle of vegetation and have forged the perspective, clothing, and language of the people.

As one heads west, crossing the Big Belt and Absaroka ranges into Gallatin County, the terrain becomes wetter and more dramatic. Gallatin County is east of the Continental Divide, yet there is sufficient rainfall here for the streams to be perennial and to support the undulating grasses of the high prairie. During the summer the saw-toothed mountains are curtained with thunderstorms, and the steep savanna turns from umber to brown. You can see the lightning strikes tracking the ridges, but you cannot hear their thunder. The storms are briefly torrential,

yet they are not enough to saturate the tinder-dry land, and the lightning sets fires. The moisture wicks quickly in the thin air and the umber returns. These highlands are distilled to a few sharp forms by altitude. A marsh hawk, narrow-winged, black with a white tail bar, soars above tawny hills. Behind it, etched in the sky, is the craggy skeleton of a blown-out limber pine. Three syllables: hawk and hill and pine. And, of course, wind, which pushes the fleeting clouds. The cloud shadows glide over the grassy mountain slopes like swarms of gnats.

View from the mountain, Flying D Ranch.

A mile high are pockets of forest known as coolies. Douglas fir and lodgepole pine were once logged in these forests, but today timber cutting has been eclipsed by the economy of valley-dwelling cattle. The coolies have once again become wild places, their understories crowded with umbels of yellow-brown cow cabbage, raspberry, yampa, and the sharp-scented silver sagebrush. Limber pines, gnarled and stunted, cling to the rocky outcroppings. They submit to the weather, bent in all manner by the crazy gusts and fraying winds that haunt the ridges. They are the wind inmaderate.

When the quaking aspens turn yellow in the autumn, the entire land seems to disassemble into a mosaic of fluttering leaves. After the deciduium, their white-and-black birchy trunks are suddenly revealed, seeming to mimic the snowy land from which they arise. In the winter, the prairie plants turn brown and crisp in the angry cold wind that prowls the plains. Some of the seeds dry in their pods and, as the wind shifts over the veldt, sound like the abrupt, shuffling footsteps of a large deer or bison. The sound startles me as I walk in the coolies, and I expect to see these animals bounding past. But there are none. It is only the hissing wind in the dormant land.

A bit north of here, in Alberta, is the terminus of a vanished migratory route from Alaska to the American plains. For 50,000 years the Wisconsin Icecap, the last of at least four glaciations during the Pleistocene, smothered most of northern America, sprawling from the Yukon south to the Great Plains, from the Pacific to the Atlantic. Several miles deep in places, the Wisconsin Icecap sequestered so much water that sea levels worldwide dropped about 360 feet, turning the Bering Sea into a land bridge between Asia and North America. The icecap was not uniform, however. Toward the beginning and toward the end of its life, an unglaciated corridor extended through it for 800 miles. Although it was as short-lived as the icecap, the corridor was one of the great biogeographic events of earth's history. Without it, the great plains of North America would not have been seeded by the waves of Asian plants, animals, and people that migrated from Siberia. Many species that are today considered quintessentially American — maples, sycamores, the extinct dire wolf, the pronghorn antelope, the raccoon, and the bison — are in fact Eurasian. Their ancestors migrated across the Bering Sea and through the interglacial corridor.

The colonizing ancestral bison species was probably the steppe bison, a massive, long-

Limber pines in a coolie.

Aspen seedlings emerging from an understory of sagebrush.

horned animal with dromedary humps that ranged from eastern Europe to the Yukon. The steppe bison repeatedly crossed the Bering land bridge into Alaska during periods of low sea level. However, the warm temperatures of the interglacial periods, which opened the ice-free corridor, also raised sea levels and closed the land bridge; for a while — perhaps for several hundred generations — the steppe bison were stranded in Alaska, unable to either return to Siberia or continue south in the Americas. By the time the southward corridor had opened and they were released, the New World bison had become substantially different from their Asian ancestors. Eventually they became a new species, the antique plains bison, which was straight-horned and small, adapted to the boom-and-bust climate of the savannas of central North America. When the last wave of steppe bison invaded Alaska eighteen thousand years ago, there was already a descendant population of antique bison on the American prairie, a relict of the penultimate ice age.

At the beginning of the ice ages, 2 million years ago, North America was emerging from a long period of isolation. (The Darién Gap, separating North and South America, closed about 2.4 million years ago. Although this event broke the isolation of North America, the migration of mammals was essentially one way, north to south. While South America was overwhelmed by North American felines and canines, only two mammals — the nine-banded armadillo and the opossum — successfully colonized North America from South America.) An island continent for at least 40 million years, North America had relatively few large ungulates, and the colonizing bison and their hybrids found a wide-open land. They quickly filled a number of empty niches that in Eurasia or Africa would have been occupied by a medley of large grazing and browsing species. Like the ancestral honeycreeper of the Hawaiian Islands, the bison radiated. As recently as 10,000 years ago, the New World bison, all descended from the steppe bison, were far more diverse than they are today: there was the large plains bison, the petite antique plains bison, and the dwarf forest bison, plus hybrids and variations of all these themes.

The mountains and prairies of western Montana have been inhabited by humans as long as any part of the United States. The ancestors of the Native Americans may have passed by here at about the same time as the last wave of bison from Alaska. (Alternatively and, it would seem, improbably, they may have traveled south by canoe along the frigid Pacific coast.) Some settled and hunted the vast herds of antique plains bison; some moved on as far as Patagonia. Others migrated to Central America, where they invented mathematics and built cities. The leavings of these first people are everywhere in western Montana: a litter of projectile points, knapped from basalt and obsidian that came from Yellowstone's Bear Gulch and, much later, from chert that was mined in the foothills of the Spanish Peaks. Today the pits of the chert mines can still be perceived, cut into the ridges and low promontories of those peaks. Nearby is a pictograph, about a thousand years old, beyond the reach of the rains under a ledge of rock. It is abstract and symbolic, a stick figure of a quadruped, painted with red hematite and blue-green celadonite. Its artist was more interested in pattern than in realism. By then the great mammals of the basins and ranges, including most types of bison, had vanished. Changes in climate and vegetation — and undoubtedly human predation — had led to their extinction. Only the North American bison, the generalist so familiar to us today, was left.

Montezuma, the Aztec king, kept a menagerie of interesting animals from various parts of his far-flung empire in his private zoo in what is now the Mexican state of Coahuila. It may have been the first zoological park in the Americas, and in its pens the Spanish *conquistadors* under the command of Hernán Cortés first encountered the North American bison. An early Spanish chronicler wrote, "It has crooked Shoulders, with a Bunch on its back like a Camel; its Flanks dry, its Tail large, and its Neck cover'd with Hair like a Lion." The Iberian writer may have found the bison a frightening apparition, but a northern European would have found it familiar. The wisent, a closely related species that was also a descendant of the Siberian steppe bison, was common in the forests of Poland and White Russia.

   At the time of the European arrival in the New World, the American bison may have been the most abundant large mammal on earth, ranging from the Pacific coast to the eastern piedmont of the Appalachians. Estimates of its numbers are as high as 60 million. The descriptions of bison herds, even as late as the nineteenth century, were astonishing. In May 1871 Colonel R. I. Dodge wrote of the bison near Fort Zara, Arkansas.

> The whole country appeared one great mass of buffalo, moving slowly to the northward; and it was only when actually among them that it could be ascertained that the apparently solid mass was an agglomeration of innumerable small herds, from fifty to two hundred animals. . . . The buffalo on the hills, seeing an unusual object in their rear, turned, stared an instant, then started at full speed directly towards me, stampeding and bringing with them the numberless herds through which they passed, and pouring down upon me all the herds, no longer separated, but one immense compact mass of plunging animals, mad with fright, and as irresistible as an avalanche.

After the Civil War, American adventurers were attracted by the fertile prairies in the heart of their country — bison country. They were children of the Industrial Revolution, and often its refugees. Most arrived by train, first as laborers who built the rail lines and later as colonists who settled in the villages strung along the iron sinews of the growing nation. The bison were a cheap and, it seemed, unlimited source of food. The railway workers and the armies that protected them from the Native Americans were provisioned by teams of professional bison hunters and skinners. In 1882 there were five thousand hunters in the northern plains alone. They produced far more meat than they could sell. Often the pelt and the fatty tongue were the only parts of the bison that were utilized; the rest of the carcass was left to rot. In *The Plains of the Great West*, William Blackmore wrote:

> In the autumn of 1868, whilst crossing the plains on the Kansas Pacific Railroad, for a distance of upwards of 120 miles, between Ellisworth and Sheridan, we passed through an almost unbroken herd of buffalo. The plains were blackened with them, and more than once the trains had to stop to allow unusually large herds to pass.

Target practice was an amusing diversion during the tedious transcontinental rail passage. Comfortably ensconced in armchairs, rifles in their laps, gentleman pioneers shot bison by the thousands from passing trains. It wasn't much of a sport; they didn't even have to suffer the inconvenience of standing up. The slain animals were left to rot where they fell, and the bones of millions accumulated along the rail lines. It was a carnage without precedent, and without premonition of its consequences.

By 1889, there were fewer than a thousand bison left in the wild in North America. In that year, William F. Hornaday wrote, "Although the existence of a few widely-scattered individuals enables us to say that the bison is not yet absolutely extinct in a wild state, there is no reason to hope that a single wild and unprotected individual will remain alive ten years hence" (p. 521). Hornaday was the chief taxidermist of the U.S. National Museum, who three years before had mounted an expedition to shoot and collect representative specimens of the last remaining bison. He was therefore personally responsible for substantially diminishing the remaining populations. Regardless, Hornaday's report convinced President Teddy Roosevelt, in 1893, to set aside widely scattered reserves to protect the remaining animals.

The vanguard of a herd of bison.

Because of Roosevelt's action, the bison survived, and not just as a graven image on the nickel. Today there are approximately 130,000 North American bison, all descended from the relict three hundred. Although their ancestors came from widely scattered populations, representing much of the diversity of North American bison, the reduction from 60 million to a few hundred animals nevertheless created a near-catastrophic genetic bottleneck. Today the descendants of the surviving bison are acutely inbred, with only a fraction of the full range of their ancestors' variation in size, fleetness, furriness, and instinct. Essentially, this has created a founder effect. Just as the limited ancestral traits of the Hawaiian honeycreeper circumscribed the adaptive spectrum of its descendants, the particular traits of the surviving bison diminished the diversity of their descendants. In a sense, no matter how abundant it becomes, the North American bison will always be a shadow-species. It is already half extinct.

After the destruction of the bison, the Great Plains changed forever. The prairie submitted to the plow, and within a hundred years it became a tri-culture of corn, soybeans, and wheat. In the arid west, bison were supplanted by cattle and sheep, and the wolves were driven to extinction. The cowboy became the symbol of the American West, a paladin of American democratic liberty.

But the stoic bison shall forever remain better suited to these plains than the upstart Middle Eastern cattle and sheep. It is well insulated and indifferent to winter storms, endowed with huge neck muscles that swing the head back and forth to break through snow and reach the forage underneath, and its digestive tract is attuned to the native plants with which it evolved for millennia. The bison, the invocation of the American prairie, does not require the introduced grasses that have displaced native species. Why, therefore, have ranchers not turned to bison instead of cattle? Why has the American palate lost its craving for bison meat and shifted to beef? The answer is the same in Montana as it is in Ecuador or Paraguay. People had to make a living from this land, and they chose the ways that they knew and that their fathers knew. Cattle were a sure thing; they were tradition. And if anything characterized the cowboy, it was tradition.

*

A bison grizzled by snow.

135

A few imaginative entrepreneurs have bucked this trend and are experimenting with bison ranching. One is Ted Turner, the owner of the 107,000-acre Flying D Ranch near Gallatin, Montana. For generations the Flying D was a conventional cattle ranch, but after Turner acquired the property in 1989, he evicted the cattle and restored the bison. Today the ranch has a standing population of 3,300 adult bison: 300 bulls and 3,000 cows, which every summer give birth to about 2,400 calves. Turner's choice was obviously beneficial to the environment and truer to an American heritage that long preceded cattle ranching. But it was also economically sound. Bison are more fecund than cattle, having a reproductive life of twenty years; by contrast, cattle reproduce for only twelve. Naturally lean, bison meat is a healthier food than beef, especially the grain-fed beef to which the American palate has become so fatally attracted. Bison meat doesn't marble, so it is even lower in fat and cholesterol than those staples of dieters, skinned chicken and turkey. In fact, it is so lean that during the winter the Plains Indians were unable to subsist on bison meat alone; they had to supplement their diet with seeds to obtain enough fat. The American palate has become more catholic as well as more health-conscious. Bison meat has become a valuable commodity. In 1989 good cuts of bison retailed for as much as twenty dollars a pound. The premium price was at least partially a function of its rarity; the entire North American bison population is roughly equivalent to the number of cattle slaughtered each weekday in the United States.

Bison are less destructive to the range than cattle. Always on the move, they eat a wider spectrum of plants than cattle and therefore use the land more fully. However, their wanderlust is an economic disadvantage. Foraging burns energy, and as a result bison calves gain weight more slowly than cattle and take longer to reach marketable size.

When Turner bought the Flying D, cattle had been raised there for so long that much of the original vegetation had disappeared. The valley floors were paved with timothy. Wild iris and silky lupine, signs of land abused by cattle, were rampant. The forested arroyos of willow and aspen had been munched to barrenness. The western side of the ranch was yoked to the production of alfalfa and other winter fodder. Richardson's ground squirrels were out of control in places, creating crystalline excrescences of urine and feces around their warrens, hiccups of disequilibrium that looked like blowouts. The eastern end of the Flying D was wilder, although much of the vegetation had shifted to a suite of introduced Eurasian species that spread easily in ground broken up by the hooves of cattle. The land that the bison came back to was, in a sense, an alien one.

Aspens above a meadow of sneezeweed in flower.

Frustratingly, the bison, just like cattle, love to eat the succulent aliens and therefore disperse them. Fire, always at home on the prairie, has helped a lot, keeping some of these species at bay and encouraging natives such as aspen, wheatgrass, and Idaho fescue. Since Turner took over the ranch, there have been regular controlled burns. But fire is the ally of several of the most persistent exotics — Japanese brome, leafy spurge, and timothy — which are adapted to the flame and have benefited from the burnings.

Sweet timothy, an alien grass adored by bison.

I spent a week on the Flying D, exploring its savannas, mountains, and coolies. In spite of years of ranching, farming, and logging, it remains an extraordinarily diverse place, with many small refuges of wilderness. It is like a private Yellowstone, sans geysers and roads thrombosed by cars. My guide was Bud Griffith, who has been a hand on the Flying D since 1959. A keen observer, Bud is one of the finest natural historians I have known. He loves the ranch as if it were his own, and he may know it better than anybody else. Bud can read changes in the land and understand their portent. Watch the cold bottoms of the canyons, he explains. That's where recovery is first noticeable. Observe how the cowed-out streams are being colonized by buttonwoods, willows, and chokecherries. The aspens, favorite browse of the elk, are returning. Beavers, which create wetlands, are moving in; their chiseled tooth marks girdle the white aspen trunks from which they build their dams. Moose, Bud explains, are also

A beaver-gnawed log.

returning to the Flying D. They are good overall indicators of recovery because they demand a healthy and diverse environment. Of all the local mammals, their population is the hardest to maintain.

Bud started out as a cowboy and wound up as a bisonboy. To prepare me to visit the bison, Bud first teaches me bison etiquette. You have to be polite around these animals, he explains. They behave more like horses than cattle and respond to tact and good manners. Never, he advises me, approach a bison head on. Dominant males are riled by confrontation; they cock their tails and may attack. You have to edge around a bison or let it approach you first. But if you're gentle and passive, a curious calf or two may approach after a while, snuffling the air and staring. At first their mothers may nuzzle them away, but eventually they will relax and ignore you. And then you become one of the herd.

On this August afternoon, the savannas of the Flying D are bowed with seed, a golden plain of protein and carbohydrate. Sweet clover, an introduced species, charges the prairie air with the succulent aroma of honey and straw. In the slanting afternoon sun, the valleys are filled with the pale glare of cheatgrass, so named because cattle won't eat it. A coyote is bounding in the tawny grass, occasionally spy-hopping to keep an eye on us. The long red guard hairs on its gray back and flanks are the exact color of the bluestems. Coyotes often associate with bison, eating the mice and ground squirrels flushed by the herd. Maybe it is hoping that we will flush some too. Instead, we alarm a clackety yellow-legged grasshopper, which jumps into the heat-stilled air.

There seems to be an inordinate number of dung-eating beetles and flies: the bison must be close. I can smell them and hear their bleatings in the valley ahead. Suddenly, as we cross a low ridge, we spot them, clumped like a brown cloud shadow in the valley below. The shape of the herd tells a lot about bison behavior, Bud explains. Bison find it comforting to see a horizon, so they stay in the center of the valley, carefully avoiding the shadowed places — mountains, trees, and canyons — where grizzlies and wolves used to hide. Although these predators are vanishingly rare today, the bison atavistically remember them. Their claustrophobia is an instinct against phantoms. On the move, the bison tend to migrate sinuously, single file. I have often wondered about this behavior, which is shared by most savanna-dwelling mammals, from the Serengeti to Montana. It may be an adaptation to poisonous snakes. Clearly, in a place where western diamondback rattlers are common, it is safest to follow in another's footsteps.

We drive the Jeep ahead of the advancing herd and wait. After a period of contemplation, the lead bison reluctantly continue. In half an hour, the herd has closed around us, conceding us a vacuole of personal space a few bison lengths in diameter. They are incessantly calling to each other. The calves have abbreviated bleats; their mothers' calls are long and guttural. We quietly observe, using our noses and ears as much as our eyes. They reek of damp fur, like wet dogs, and of warm dung. The herd seems possessed by switching and twitching. Their sheeting back muscles solidly tug their furry mantles, arousing clouds of flies that almost immediately alight again. A heifer stoops on her shins to rub her dewlap on a mound of dirt. Then she sidles onto her back, shoving each side of her dorsal ridge onto the mound. The ridge prevents her from completely rolling over. Now two calves mimic the adults and begin to roll. Another heifer delicately inserts a back hoof into her itchy ear and closes her eyes with pleasure. A large black calf bounds to his mother's udder and enthusiastically nudges her teats.

He is so tall that he must hunch down on his elbows; he sucks so enthusiastically that white milk froths around his mouth. Clearly irritated by her weanling, the mother raises a leg and expertly pushes him away.

Most of the calves were born within a forty-five day period, beginning in April. Gestation in bison lasts nine months, and since a cow produces a calf every year, she spends three quarters of her adult life pregnant and half of her life lactating. Three months after giving birth she comes into estrus. The bulls, at the peak of their rut, become randy and aggressive. But on this day in late August, exhausted from the travail of lust, they disdain the herd, with its frisky and clamorous infants. Now solitary and aloof, they are as still and as dark as kopjes. The calves grow rapidly in the fruiting plain. After two to three months they shed their juvenile coats, the reddish color of the spring grass. At first only their muzzles turn dark. Later, like a change of season, the brown pelage of maturity spreads over the rest of their bodies.

A scene from times past: a vast herd of bison.

We are immersed in bison for most of the lingering afternoon. At dusk the heat is broken by a thunderstorm that has been threatening from behind the mountains for hours, reverberating like an earthquake. Beneath storm clouds fissured by the setting sun, we retreat to the mountains. The storm is mostly dry, with a billowing wind redolent of damp earth, dung, and sweet clover. The bison are skittish. Are they frequently struck by lightning? Do the bison, so wed to the open plain for fear of wolves, instead suffer the indifferent predation of electricity? At dusk the storm converts to a cold drizzle. The valley is wrapped in darkness. The bison are invisible, but I can hear them bleating, and I can smell them.

A bison calf and its mother.

The Río San Pedro

The Difference That Water Makes

ALL DURING THE WINTER of 1992–93, the Valley of the San Pedro River was an oasis, fed by long rains that tumbled across the Mojave and Sonoran deserts from the Pacific. The monsoons were presaged by light clouds and a clear dry wind, redolent with mesquite and creosotebush. On the second day the clouds looked bruised, and by the third day they hung low and expectant with rain. Slowly the sky dissolved in a steady drizzle that lasted a week. Soaking up this slow draft, the land became two-tiered: the pale-flowered ocotillos floated above the mesquites, which, darkened by oozing sap, appeared charred by fire. By spring the long rains had become intermittent, and then they stopped.

On June 22, after three months without rain, the San Pedro River abruptly disappeared. For the rest of the summer, short, violent Mexican storms would briefly resurrect it. As in Montana, these lightning storms, in spite of their torrential rains, set fire to the desert tinder, then triggered flash floods. You could hear the rumble of the floodwaters, the bashing debris, the angry clatter of pebbles echoing on the canyon walls, long before the water arrived. In an hour, perhaps a day, it abated, and the point bars and tangled banks of the San Pedro were awash with reddish foam, mats of debris, flocculent grass seeds, and the buoyant trunks of trees.

Today, in mid-October, the San Pedro is restored. I am watching phoebes hunt in the willow-shaded understory of a point bar. The southern sides of the willow trunks, which faced the torrents of summer, are caked with mud. On the gravel embankment a blue-throated hummingbird tips its beak into the corolla of a railroad vine. The bird's iridescence seems artificial, changing its reflectance as it turns its head and ruffles its feathers in the strong desert sunlight. Opposite the deep-cut meanders are moraines of silt as smooth as slate, bristling with year-old seedlings of cottonwoods and tamarisks and traversed by the tri-toed tracks of a great blue heron. The copse of elfin trees is like a field of coarse grass. Probably none of the seedlings will survive to adulthood; indeed, most will wash away in the next flood.

The trees on this shifting riverbank have short, fast-growing lives: a fifty-foot cottonwood may be no more than ten years old. The tamarisks, weeds from Eurasia that are displacing the native trees, do much better. Capable of regenerating from scraps and mangled shards of roots, they seem to survive almost any beating that the river can present.

The Río San Pedro is born as a stream in the Ajos and Mariquitas mountains of northern Mexico, in the state of Sonora. Its beginnings, beneath the pall of the copper smelter near the city of Canancas, are uninspiring. The plumes of the plant's stacks are visible for forty miles across the Sonoran Desert. Its acid precipitation has singed the southeastern flank of the Mariquitas, leaving them with a stubble of barren pines. Now and then the plant vomits liquid tailings laced with heavy metals, which leak into the river, essentially sterilizing it. By the time the San Pedro reaches the U.S. border, it is clear, very often acidic, and nearly devoid of life.

The San Pedro crosses the border as a stream a few yards wide just west of Bisbee, Arizona, meanders through savanna and desert scrub west and north of the mining town of Tombstone, and eases north along the western flanks of the Mule and Galiuro mountains. The valley is shaded by solitary willows and cottonwoods, the aeries of zone-tailed hawks. Farther north, the San Pedro carves its own tapering canyon, the Aravaipa, before entering the Gila River.

The Gila, in turn, is a tributary of the Colorado River, which, after being robbed by the city of Los Angeles, returns to Mexico and debouches into the Gulf of California.

The San Pedro, a rambling and fickle island of water in the desert, is in many aspects as different from its ambient as Moloka'i is distinct from the Pacific. It is a green and silver conduit of life, a pathway from the subtropical basins and ranges of Mexico to the southern Rockies of the United States. Three hundred and sixty-seven species of birds, including such rarities as the southwest willow flycatcher, green kingfisher, gray hawk, Mississippi kite, and tropical kingbird, use the San Pedro as a migratory corridor.

For most of its length the San Pedro is intermittent. In certain basins it vanishes, simply seeping into the sand. But where a tributary enters the river, or its valley is partially blocked by a beaver dam or is paved with sandstone, the San Pedro dilates into cool, shallow pools resounding with the calls of bullfrogs. These are the *ciénagas* (marshes) and *bosques* (riparian woods), starkly defined by cattails, sedges, and tall fringing stands of cottonwoods. From a distance, they look like black striations on the tawny land. They are the first perennial places on the San Pedro, life rafts in the desert during the dry season: 80 to 85 percent of Arizona's animal species directly or indirectly depend on them.

*

The lower San Pedro River as it passes the Galiuro Mountains near Kielberg Canyon.

Water, this light-footed nomad, seems as ephemeral as a cloud here. Since the European arrival in the 1500s, the American Southwest has lost 85–90 percent of its wetlands. Once thirteen species of fish were endemic to the San Pedro. Now only two survive. Today the ground-water level at Tucson, sixty miles west of the San Pedro, is 365 feet below the surface of the desert. At the turn of the century it was 14 feet down. The control and management of water are equivalent to money and power in the desert Southwest. The San Pedro is strangling. In the middle of a sea of Bermuda grass, between the Dobbin and Reese ranches along the river, there are twenty-four irrigation wells. When the pumps are turned on, the ground water races toward the wells like rabbits to a hole, and the whole land changes. The question today is whether the San Pedro will survive at all. The quality of its water will become irrelevant if there is no quantity.

It would be facile to attribute the decline entirely to humans. The desert Southwest has experienced dramatic climate changes, quite independent of human activities, since the end of the Wisconsin Ice Age, 12,000 years ago. About a thousand years later, humans arrived in the San Pedro River Valley. They were the Clovis people, hunter-gatherers who left the first unequivocal human traces in North America. Like the animals they hunted, the Clovis people tended to follow rivers, and there are more Clovis sites along the San Pedro River than any other place in Arizona. Murray Springs, an eroded creek edge shaded by desert willows in the flatlands west of the Mule Mountains, is the most important Clovis site. Its sediments hide the remains of eleven mammoths, as well as bison, tapir, and camel. Here archaeologists discovered the front half of a human-made stone projectile embedded in the leg bone of a mammoth; the back half was found in a nearby campsite. It may have been the smoking gun. All of these large mammals went extinct at about the time of the Clovis people or shortly after. The question whether humans caused their demise or they succumbed to changes in climate is a subject of great debate among scholars. The answer is probably both. In any event, until about 4,000 years ago the San Pedro was a perennial, marshy river, and its valley was laced with oak woodlands. It was, in essence, a giant *bosque.*

The second major anthropogenic change came to the land about 2,400 years ago. It was brought by the Hohokam, the first agriculturists and therefore the first sedentary people of the San Pedro Valley. The Hohokam built their homesteads on the western piedmonts of the Huachuca Mountains and seduced a few wild plants — corn, beans, and relatives of the tomato — into domestication in the fields surrounding their villages.

Blooming mustard and irrigated alfalfa, lower San Pedro River.

The traces of those settlements can still be seen today. None of the villages was self-sufficient. The settled life for the Hohokam and their successors necessitated exchange with other communities, and the river was the natural trade route. Today every flash flood releases pottery shards and pieces of shell from the concave riverbanks, proof of the duration and magnitude of this commerce.

History, both archaeological and oral, has become more explicit during the last thousand years. Between 1275 and 1290 the San Pedro Valley suffered a great drought, and the river vanished for most of the year. Many settlements had to be abandoned. During the late 1300s the Apaches, hunter-gatherers from the north, invaded the river valley. At first they pillaged the farming communities, but eventually they married the local people, settled down, and learned agriculture from them.

The Spanish arrived in the San Pedro Valley in 1536. The first *conquistadors* to cross the river reported savannas with grass so tall that a man could lose the horizon while

A mesquite bosque, Cascabel Clayworks, lower San Pedro River.

riding on horseback. Enticed by the reports, Iberian pioneers soon followed. Inevitably, they brought their sheep. The colonists built thick-walled wattle houses with small windows, which stayed cool in the summer and were easy to defend. The Spanish outposts never amounted to much, however, because the Apaches, who took readily to the Spanish horse, enthusiastically resisted the European settlers, and because malaria, carried by the abundant *Anopheles* mosquitoes, was rampant in the *ciénagas*. But the Spanish sheep, already adapted to extracting a living from the denuded parts of Iberia, were like a plague of locusts. They brought along two aggressive Eurasian weeds — foxtail (sometimes known as red brome) and mouse barley — as hitchhiking seeds in their wool. Both grasses were ideally suited to the sheep-scuffed land and displaced the edible native grasses. In most places only the most unpleasant-tasting forbs, such as sagebrush, which is protected by pungent and disagreeable oils, survived grazing. This is how the desert acquired its characteristic aroma.

Bingham Cienéga, lower San Pedro River.

Accounts from as late as the 1850s describe luxuriant grasslands and vast *ciénagas* in the San Pedro Valley. But by then, the river valley was declining. After the Apaches were pacified in 1872, the valley underwent an economic boom. Arizona had become a territory of the newly industrializing United States, which demanded silver from the mines in Tombstone and copper from those in Bisbee. The railroad arrived in 1881. It was not the mines themselves that changed the land, although they were locally devastating; it was overgrazing and the cutting of wood for heating and smithing. The preferred fuel species — indeed, the only abundant tree species — were lowland mesquite, cottonwood, and the upland pines. In ten years, 4 million cords of wood were burned to heat houses in Tombstone alone. After the local forests were cut, loggers began seeking wood deep inside Mexico. The charcoal-fired copper smelters of Bisbee, perched above an abiotic open pit, consumed an entire watershed. In the 1890s Bisbee was the largest city between St. Louis and San Francisco, but it was not a place of enlightenment. A brutal mining town, it had numerous saloons and bordellos, but no department of public education.

Large-scale ranching started at about the same time. The burgeoning population had an insatiable appetite for beef, and the cattle that were not consumed locally were easily exported by train to markets east and west. By 1891 there were 150,000 cattle and probably even more sheep in Cochise County, which encompasses the southern third of the San Pedro River Valley. The land was already marginal for grazing. During the great drought of 1891, 75 percent of the cattle of Cochise County died. The 1890s were the years of the "great downcutting," the erosion of the desert land by the lacerating hooves of cattle and by overgrazing. As the grass was removed, the color, texture, and hydrology of the land changed. The desert could no longer absorb the summer rain and instead expelled it as flash floods. Lowland mesquite invaded the deforested highlands, their seeds carried in the guts of cattle. Scarified and deposited in a pile of dung, the mesquite seeds began life in the best of all possible worlds. The scars of the downcutting are still visible today: the fissured red land, the paucity of grasses, the abundance of sharp-scented forbs that cattle disdain. The San Pedro River Valley had become a wounded landscape.

Today much of the valley belongs to the federal government and is managed by the Department of the Interior's Bureau of Land Management. Tracts of land held in public trust are leased to the local ranchers for use by their cattle and sheep. Grazing is permitted on 270 million acres of federal land in the American West, but the laissez-faire days are over. Quotas, in terms of animal unit months (AUM), restrict the density of grazing animals, depending on local circumstances and the condition of the land. One AUM is defined as a cow and her calf or five sheep. Although the AUMs, at least to some extent, protect the health of the land, the federal grazing fees have little to do with economic common sense. For decades the fees on federal lands have ranged from $1.61 to $2.36 per AUM, while fees on private lands are close to $9 per AUM. The revenues from the grazing fees do not even cover the cost of administering the properties. In essence, the government is subsidizing ranching in the West — a kind of rural welfare — by artificially maintaining an economy and way of life that otherwise would collapse under the weight of their own inefficiency.

Even with the federal subsidies, ranching is declining in the San Pedro Valley, as the browse deteriorates and the water table retreats. Many of the largest ranches are too thirsty and therefore too costly to maintain, but they are too expensive to be sold to a single buyer. As a result, they are being subdivided into 160- and 80-acre plots as homesteads and vacation retreats. The desert is turning suburban. Arizona has been discovered as a haven for retirees and tourists. New cities are appearing in the wilderness like groves of tamarisk. Today 35,000 people live in Sierra Vista, a reticulate urban sprawl on the western side of the San Pedro, where a quarter century ago there were a few roadside stores and a gas station. The large-scale perspective requisite to caring for marginal lands no longer exists. Now planners and conservationists have to deal with ten or twenty owners rather than one. The Arizona Nature Conservancy has had to expand its traditional role of acquiring land to include educating, cajoling, and advising the small landholders, inducting them into the big picture. The Conservancy has become a stable center in this disassembly.

The goal of conservation in the San Pedro Valley is, ultimately, elusive. Conservationists seek restoration, but to what? The land and vegetation here have been changing since the Pleistocene, in part because of natural processes, in part because of humans. Restoration, therefore, seeks a moving target. Neither the *bosques* nor the grasslands may be considered pristine. Upland mesquite has replaced the original pines. The tamarisk that has replaced the native riparian trees now provides nesting habitat for endangered birds, such as the willow flycatcher, that otherwise might perish. Cattle and sheep ranching have become ingrained in the local economy and psyche. The community we are restoring may not be the original, but one of our own design that suits our objectives today, an accommodation to history and to chance that is brand-new.

*

Tamarisk, a Eurasian exotic.

Souza Wash, San Pedro River.

In the hard light of a stifling October afternoon, I drive fifty miles along the Aravaipa Canyon, sculpted by the river of the same name, a tributary of the San Pedro. The dirt road enters the wide southern mouth of the canyon and meanders in tandem with the river past banks entangled with debris and the long ropy roots of cottonwoods. Their leaves, just turning yellow today, flutter like aspen leaves in the canyon wind. The canyon bottom is flat, smoothed by the sediments of flash floods. Toward the narrow end of the canyon are close, pink cliffs verdigrised with bright green lichens. Prickly pears cling to the rock shelves, reaching their mittened hands into the void. On the plateau the inflorescence of an agave — in the same genus as henequen — stabs the sky. The canyon floor is dark by midafternoon, and for a long moment only the rim stays bright. A bighorn ram stands there, stoic, feeling invulnerable on the heights. At first I see only his white rump patch in the shadows. Only later do I perceive the rest of the animal, the color of the rock itself. The ram is endowed with huge, grotesquely curved horns and the thick neck necessary to bear them. He uses them to defend his near-vertical territory against other males. I can't imagine lugging those burdens along the cliff faces. Real estate, I conclude, must be highly valuable in this reluctant land.

At the northern, narrow end of the canyon is a cliff dwelling, dating from about 1300, formed from orange mud and tucked into the overhanging north face. It enjoys the winter sun and the summer shade. Perhaps only a dozen rains have reached it in the last seven hundred years. The dwelling has a wood-linteled door half as tall as a man and no windows. The straw-reinforced wattle looks as if it had been smoothed yesterday. I place my hand in the channels molded by the fingers of its creator.

The Arizona Nature Conservancy has purchased small parcels of land in the Aravaipa Canyon and maintains a ranch house for guests here. The house is surrounded by a rambling balcony overlooking a lawn shaded by spreading pecan trees and a flowering lantana, a pungent-leafed exotic shrub from Central America. The lantana attracts a swarm of green pierid butterflies, honeybees, and spider-eating *Pepsis* wasps. A hesperid skipper, as tawny as the desert, clatters from flower to bough and surprises a mourning cloak resting quietly on a shaded leaf. She suddenly opens her wings, revealing shocking blue eyespots. In the open desert, surprise is a very effective defense.

At around midnight, the house fills with the sharp-sour smell of body odor, of musk. I sneak onto the porch and, under a cold crescent moon, watch a pack of javelinas as they crack the fallen pecans. They are grunting to each other, low-frequency vibrations of contentment that sound like stomach rumbles. This is how the herd keeps in touch. This is what binds javelina society.

The Aravaipa's native chubs have not yet been displaced by alien fish species. The water is perennial here, and it has been so long enough for the fish to have become specialized to this stretch of river, to have become endemic. I am determined to see this last refuge of riverine Arizona firsthand, the habitat of some of the rarest fish in North America. Putting on a mask and snorkel, I slide into the river where it crosses the road. The water is painfully cold and as clear as air. The current is so strong that I have to hold on to the bright pink roots of an undercut willow. The tumbling rocks of the river bottom are assorted according to size, and the eddy generated by my body has caused a flurry of pebbles to tumble down the creek bed. The chubs, only a few inches long, are as smooth as pebbles and just about as abundant. They use their ventral suckers to cling to the rocks, fins plastered to their sides to present the lowest profile to the current. Their rubber-lipped mouths are working hard, scraping algae from the rock surfaces. Their survival must be a perpetual race against the current, which makes everything more costly, even staying in place. If a chub lets go, it relinquishes the only place in the world where it can make a living.

South of Aravaipa Canyon, in the sheep-munched foothills of the Galiuro Mountains, is the Muleshoe Ranch. In 1980 the Arizona Nature Conservancy purchased the ranch outright, a total of 49,000 acres, of which only 5,800 are deeded. The rest is federal land, rented from the BLM and the U.S. Forestry Service. The Nature Conservancy pays the government the equivalent value of the AUMs that the land could support, even though it removed all the cattle from the ranch in 1980. The Muleshoe was left to recover, free of Middle Eastern mammals, and to revert to whatever quasi-native community of plants could be established after years of grazing. To the Muleshoe's neighbors, removing federal land from the local economy was a threat to western ranching traditions. The ranchers sued the Conservancy, demanding that the land be returned to "traditional" use.

The Muleshoe Ranch is graced with seven major perennial riverine areas, whose names reveal the character of the place: Hotsprings Canyon, Bass Creek, Double River Creek, Wildcat Creek, Swamp Springs Creek, and Redfield Creek. The seventh area, unnamed, is an artesian geothermal spring that pours scalding water, 105–108 degrees F, into a shallow pond, part of which is diverted into a hot tub for visitors to the ranch.

Even in the pond's hadean environment, life — ever optimistic — persists. Shelves of cyanobacteria intercept and scatter the first shafts of morning light. A few spiders skip across the pond on their tapered leg-tips from snag to snag, as fast as they can walk on the surface tension. Too fast and they sink; too slow and they poach. In the cool of dawn, heat-charged by the spring, they become active sooner than their stiff-jointed prey. A male damselfly is darning his mate on the wing. With him still clasped to the back of her neck, she futilely sows her eggs in the scalding water.

Later in the morning I walk down the flat-bottomed wash. My face and hands burn in the autumn sun, yet the early morning air is still cold. In the direction of the sun, white dust scatters the light into a column. A male fence lizard with metallic blue scales does pushups on the brown, warming rocks. The riverbed sediments have been consolidated by the tenacious wash flora. Behind each forb is a wake of sand deposited by the last flash flood. The vegetation is thorny, scabrous, and diminutive of leaf. The pale wolfberry bushes are bearing red fruits today. They have tapering, spinelike twigs, which themselves have spines, the

The San Pedro Riparian National Conservation Area.

woody, long-lived defenses of a slow-growing plant, an investment in permanence. Purple-rayed daisies appear to have an internal radiance in the shade, but in full sun they are invisible. A split cottonwood trunk, its asymmetric growth rings crafted by the shifting strains and currents that once washed over it, is splayed across the wash. Short-lived, with soft and spongy wood, it will decompose quickly. How articulate is this broken log, its cuneiform bark disheveled by the absent river. A pair of pyrrhuloxias, pale relatives of cardinals, are peering into the open center of the log. A tassel-eared squirrel, with tufted ears, also investigates, snuffling under the peeling bark.

Ahead, in the grassy, soft shade of a spreading Arizona hazelnut, is an oasis. A blue magnificent hummingbird alights on a low twig. Its sweet feces, accumulating beneath the hazelnut, attract an occasional insect. When a wasp decides to investigate the source of this bounty, the hummingbird fends it off with a scimitar wing, rises, then alights and preens. Two wings, it seems, are swifter and more adroit than four.

The desert has an olfactory clarity: the sharp, startling, terpene aroma of one-seed juniper, the stench of putrefaction rising on the thermals, the wet-mineral smell under a rock in the dry riverbed. The desert air also is transparent to sound. I notice that the frequency of the crickets' chirping increases as the day warms. I can hear the roar of a fly and, from clear across the wash, the pattering of a hundred butterfly wings surrounding a bleeding mesquite like a flurry of flower petals. The voice of a raven, turning on invisible thermals, rasps through the canyon. I can hear its feathers sliding like silk; the forlorn call of a mourning dove; the thunking of a gila woodpecker; the staccato clicking of a grasshopper as it gathers the wet oozings of the punctured mesquite. A group of Gambel's quails, bustling down the dry riverbed, pauses, momentarily alert. Then, in unison, they resume foraging. One, aloof, stands sentinel.

Palau

The Edge of the Void

THE SEA ABOVE IS AS TRANSPARENT AS WIND. Peering upward through the water into the canopy of bright air, I watch the silhouette of a flying fox — a fruit-eating bat with the wingspan of a small eagle — gliding as if among the spreading sea fans and a school of neon damselfish. That, of course, is an illusion. The bat is flying between the crowns of the shaggy *Casuarina* trees that overhang the Rock Islands of Palau; below, in the tide-washed channel where the sea dances with plankton, the pastel sea fans swoon in the current from which they filter their dinner.

At Palau the floor of the western Pacific rises abruptly from the cerulean depths. The magnitude of this flooded mountaintop, the pervasive sky, is disquieting. Even from far across the water the low-hanging clouds reflect the sea's green or the shadows of land. The shallow water along the margins of the islands is incandescent turquoise, alarmingly bright when seen from the deck of a ship. The Palauan mariners can read the depth of the water from its hue; the pale sand flats beckon safety, but each shadowed reef portends danger — and opportunity.

Palau, where tropical forests grow in voluptuous proximity to coral reefs, is like no other place on earth. It is a dispersed archipelago of 340 islands, volcanic nubbins on the western edge of Micronesia, extending from Helen Reef, 150 miles off the coast of New Guinea, to Ngeruangel, 510 miles to the northeast and halfway to Guam. There is plenty of wilderness here; Palau's population is only 16,000. Most of the islands, including the multifarious Rock Islands, are inside the vast Koror Lagoon, which embraces about a thousand square miles from Peleliu Island to the northern tip of Babeldoab Island. Babeldoab, the largest island, has extensive freshwater streams that originate in tropical forest and debouch into the lagoon, flooding it with the nutrients the reef requires. The western side of the island is a mosaic of estuaries, fringing reefs, lagoons, isolated bommies that rise from the sandy sea floor, sea-grass beds, and mud flats where the tide abandons the buried fauna for half the day — a variety of habitats that sustains an extravagant diversity of species.

During the summer, the intertropical convergence zone, a globe-girdling trough of low pressure, sweeps north of the archipelago, and the wet trade winds shift from northeasterly to westerly. Twelve hundred years ago the ancestors of the Palauans took advantage of this sea change and sailed to the archipelago from Indonesia and the Philippines in open canoes. Not surprisingly, most of Palau's plants and animals, both terrestrial and marine, arrived by the same route, drifting as planktonic larvae on the prevailing currents or wafting on the monsoonal winds from the Philippine archipelago, Indonesia, and New Guinea. A minority of species arrived from the islands and shoals to the east of Palau: Yap, the Carolines, and the Marshalls, which are even more isolated and where the speciation that is characteristic of islands intensifies. Palau, therefore, is a crossroads, with most of its species borrowed from other places. The shallow sea around the archipelago is the epicenter of fish diversity in the western Pacific. Some 96 percent of the identified species of Micronesian fish — about a thousand species — occur here; that is 35 percent of all the inshore fish of the Indo-Pacific, a vast biogeographic area that extends from the Red Sea to Hawaii. On the other hand, very few of its species are unique. A recent survey in Palau revealed 136 newly recorded fish, but none were new species.

In their interiors the Rock Islands harbor secret, steep-walled lakes, where cold, fresh rain water has percolated through the spongy rock, making the ocean water fresh and chilly on top, hot and salty beneath — an inverted thermocline. Here the soft corals and sea fans, their blades strategically splayed across the current, intercept and devour the living tide. Some of the soft corals are albino, perhaps bleached of their zooxanthellae by the low temperatures. *Cassiopeia* jellyfish flop upside down on the sandy bottom, presenting their green, frilly tentacles to the light above. Their strategy is to rest on the lake floor rather than expend energy pulsing to the inconstant sea surface. The most extraordinary Palauan lake is in the heart of Eli Malk Island, surrounded by a forested ridge where the fruit doves mournfully call.

A top-heavy rock island in Koror Lagoon.

The Rock Islands, where forest meets reef.

You enter the lake in the muddy shallows, between the mangrove roots, and swim gently to its center, so as not to mix the rain-fed lens of fresh water with the salt water below. The lake has been isolated for millennia and has evolved two species of rust-colored jellyfish which occur in uncountable numbers of all sizes. Each has a cross of mesentery in its bell, which undulates and tugs the gonad-stuffed tentacles, lumpy with eggs. Like the *Cassiopeias,* they are peacefully invaded by photosynthetic commensal algae. The jellyfish follow the sun across the face of sky, making brief forays into the sunlit brackish lens, then sinking to restore their osmotic balance.

In a gray monsoonal rain, I enter the mangrove-lined Ngetpang River, which runs through the heart of Babeldoab Island. The canopy almost closes over the river. We are in the Boston Whaler of Captain Bena Sakuma, a Palauan whose ancestors have fished and hunted in Koror Lagoon for centuries and who knows it as well as any living person. Red mangrove trees, supported by arched flying buttresses 15 feet high, overhang the river, bearing bright red viviparous seeds. In the Indo-Pacific, mangroves of the genus *Brugeria* occupy the zone where black mangroves would grow in the tropical Atlantic. *Brugeria* mangroves have strong, flat, wavy pneumatophores, which are carved by the Palauans into storyboards. Prized by collectors as objects of art, the storyboards are accounts of the colonization of the islands, of typhoons and settlement, the Palauans' heritage.

A ten-foot-long saltwater crocodile has worn a smooth patch in the mud among the pneumatophores. The saltwater crocodile, which ranges from Australia to Micronesia, is the largest crocodile species on earth. Some reach twenty feet, although this croc would be lucky to grow to half that length before being shot by a hunter. The color of mud, it rests quietly on the clay bank, gauging our intentions. A skitter of mangrove crabs, aroused by our wake, tumble across the mud and climb the bank on pointed legs. One clambers over the tail of the crocodile; the two animals seem indifferent to each other. The female crabs have swollen aprons. In a few days, at the full moon, they will march to the sea in a leggy tide that seems to give the land a moving skin. The females have one overwhelming imperative: to dip their aprons into the sea and release their eggs in the ebbing tide. For a night or two one won't be able to walk in northern Babeldoab without crushing them.

The crocodile lingers on the bank until the last minute, then, realizing that our boat will not relent, slides into the channel. A few miles upstream, the sudden presence of *Nipa* palms tells us that the freshwater lens has reached the river bottom. The mangroves, deprived of the

Saltwater crocodiles.

advantage of salt water, compete poorly in the tropical forest and quickly decline. Beyond this point everything changes; the landscape is crowded with terra firma trees living in a mosaic of light gaps of different ages and sizes. This heterogeneous environment is far more diverse than the mangrove-dominated margin of the island.

We return to the coast in the late afternoon on an ebbing tide. The water at the mouth of the river is turbid and appears wormy from the mix of salinities. As in Guaraqueçaba and Florida Bay, microscopic particles are being swept into the sea; the productivity of the land is transferred to the ocean by means of detritus coated with marine fungi. The marine community at the estuary mouth responds to this bonanza and supports as great a diversity of corals as is found anywhere else on earth.

*

Four hundred species of stony corals and two hundred species of soft corals have been counted in Palau's archipelago, approximately ten times the number of coral species found in the West Indies. But the true number is not yet fully known. The Indo-Pacific coral species are notoriously plastic, assuming radically different morphologies as a function of the light, depth, and currents where they settled as larvae. Therefore, to the great

confusion of taxonomists, the morphologies of coral inevitably exceed the number of species. Inducted into the underwater realm in the West Indies, I have never seen reefs as tiered and structured as these in Palau. I never imagined that there were so many ways to reach for the light and the plankton.

I spend most of the daylight hours diving in the lagoon west of Babeldoab, gliding

A natural bridge in the Rock Islands.

over the corals and sea grasses, gaining little snippets of information. All are fleeting images: the furtive eye of the hind (a small relative of the groupers) in a cave, a stalk-eyed hermit crab lurching into its borrowed shell, a cowering squirrelfish, the arrogant neon display of a blue damsel. Giant clams evert their mantle-lips to the sky. Like the corals, they are inoculated with algae that grab the sun's energy. These, and countless other encounters, all add up to a narrative, a tapestry, and, eventually, understanding. It takes many dives before the story begins to make sense. The little details are the language of the reef, which, like all languages, is learned one word at a time; the syntax and sentence structure come later.

The shallow flats of the lagoon, jostled twice daily by tides and bashed every few years or so by a typhoon, favor the sea grasses, branching sponges, sea fans, and gorgonians, which, like a bamboo forest in the wind, are strong but yielding. A pair of vertical knifefish, so elongated that they can swim only backward, mimic the strands of sea grass. Pushed by a long ventral fin, they swim in pulses, wait, and, if the coast is clear, pulse again. A school of gray, mottled goatfish are tapping their barbels on the sand; another is watching a hole, waiting for its edible occupant to appear. Like a boa constrictor in the branches of a tree, a long-snouted, prehensile-tailed pipefish gropes from gorgonian to gorgonian, searching for prey with protruding eyes that move independently.

In the most tranquil parts of the lagoon, in the leeward sides of the channels, are nubbined stands of *Porites* coral. Each nub bears pale scars from the nips of butterflyfish and parrotfish. Here also are the staghorn corals, like heaps of broken icicles. From a distance, in the bouncing, percolating light, a vast colony of staghorn coral appears hemispherical, but up close I perceive that it is a tangle of branches. Their growing tips are incandescent purple, not yet colonized by the zooxanthellae borne by the older polyps. Legions of matching purple damselfish hide in the branches, seeming to merge with the coral. The bicolored hogfish, blennies, and damselfish take their camouflage a step further: where light and shadow are the recurring motifs, they have neon-blue heads that mimic the bright sunlit sea and brown or deep blue posteriors like the recesses of the shaggy corals into which they insert their tails.

A small wrasse solicits passersby from the meanders of an overhanging brain coral. Here, as in the tropical Atlantic, its coloration — horizontal black and white stripes — signals that it is a cleaning fish, adapted to picking external parasites from the skin and gills of larger fish and thus receiving carte blanche from predators.

Schooling fish (mostly sergeant majors) on a patch reef.

Where two corals of different species meet, one overgrows the other in a necrotic black wave. Reef-building corals have veritable pecking orders, enforced by digestive enzymes and chemicals that they excrete into the water. Therefore, whenever possible, each coral fastidiously avoids touching another — a cringe frozen in stone — in order to avoid confrontation.

On the far edge of the lagoon, depth rapidly filters out the light and its life-endowing energy. The deep sea suffocates her children. The lower reef, shaded by the growing canopy of corals, is overgrown by foliating algae. A black-and-white Moorish idol, with an arching scimitar dorsal fin, passes by like a ribbon cut loose in the wind. A hawksbill turtle, the size of a pizza, is browsing on tunicates under a shelf of coral. Its shell scatters shafts of sunlight just as the dark water does. The nocturnal, light-phobic cardinalfish and squirrelfish dwell here beneath overhanging rocks. They withdraw from sight as I glide overhead. A cobalt-blue *Linkia* starfish reaches two of its legs into a cranny. Below, a brown moray eel, his nares protruding like two tiny siphons, pokes his craggy face out of a crevice in the reef. He turns to face me, then, thinking again, withdraws.

The narrative continues; a lifetime isn't enough time to read it all. There are more words in this reef than in the language I speak.

Last February, March, and April, at the full moon, many of the fish, shrimps, crabs, and lobsters migrated to the edge of the open sea to spawn. At a depth of 60 to 120 feet, all manner of fish that spend their adult lives on the reef congregated by the thousands, turning in the sea like swarms of autumn leaves, and released their eggs and milt into the prevailing currents. Tens of thousands of orange, white, and black pyramid butterfly fish schooled just beyond the wall. Yellow and black male wrasses darted after the females as they extruded their eggs into the water. Each female released hundreds, thousands, perhaps even millions of diminutive eggs. Everybody was taking a chance. Predatory fish, which like guerrilla fighters attack from the safety of the corals, risked swimming to the fringe of the lagoon to feast on the eggs and larvae. For a few days the lagoon appeared abandoned. Most of the eggs and larvae, of course, were eaten by the ravenous tide. Why do all these fish lay their eggs in the open sea, when the chances of the offspring returning to the reef are negligible? The answer is that there is no space for small fry on the crowded reef, whereas the ocean has food and unlimited elbow room. The high mortality there is irrelevant. In the end, all that is necessary for the population to remain stable is for each pair of fish to replace itself.

Today, in mid-July, the reefs and ocean lakes of the Rock Islands have become nurseries.

The sea is dusted with the light-scattering larvae of all the returning fry, the unlikely survivors of the perils of infancy. Now is the moment of metamorphosis. All these babies are radically changing their morphologies and behaviors to adapt to adult life among the corals. The larval crabs, shrimps, and lobsters develop walking legs and pincers; the semitransparent larval fish adopt the colors of the reef or of territorial flags.

The edge of the reef, where the rocks reach for the sun.

This fish-bright tide has another extraordinary trait: almost all of the incoming juveniles are females. And most will remain female throughout their lives, members of the harem of a dominant male. A few, however, will become males in middle age, after the demise of the dominant — and highly territorial — male on their little patch of reef. His presence socially and hormonally suppresses this transformation; his absence releases it. Sequential hermaphroditism is characteristic of more than 80 percent of the reef fish of Palau. Swimming over this crowded lagoon, I can see why this behavior — so unorthodox among other animals — is so prevalent here. Certainly it is safer for a youngster to enter the crowded reef as an innocuous female, welcome in the harem of a feisty, dominant male who will struggle to maintain a patch of real estate where she can grow to maturity in safety, than as a male challenging a territory-holding individual.

*

The moon seems almost to reach to the earth here, as if this were a binary planet. Its reflection in the soothed sea seems almost palpable, and on this night in late July, the moon — almost full — fills the sea with a cold blue light. A night dive is perceptually more piecemeal than a day dive. You have to concentrate on orientation while being bucked by the waves and tugged by the inexorable current. The sweeping beam of the dive light provides only fleeting information, yet it reveals startling colors that are never visible during the day, for the deep water filters out the full spectrum of the sunlight. Night brings a changing of the guard. On the rim of my vision is a fleet of squids. I can see only their huge iridescent eyes, adapted to soaking up the moonlight of the sea surface. The promontories of sponge and coral are festooned with the extended arms of green and brown crinoids, relatives of sea stars, which by day are hunched into nondescript balls. Among the interstices of coral, the dive light catches the red-ember eyes of shrimp as they remove little morsels of algae with pincers as delicate as forceps. Pencil-spined sea urchins also graze on the patches of algae. The polyps of the stony corals, which are folded by day, reach their tentacles into the sea to feed on the night plankton and the larval offspring of their neighbors. The beam of my light is a photon trap that attracts the animal plankton like moths to a flame. It becomes a bright column of swirling food; I splash it across the hungry corals and watch the polyps close on the bounty.

Like the fish of Koror Lagoon, the corals time their reproduction according to the rhythm of the tide-drawn sea. The lunar cycle is etched into their genes; not knowing it would be fatal. A few species of corals reproduce by budding, and several brood their young, releasing their fertilized eggs only after they have matured, but most are hermaphrodites that jettison eggs and sperm into the sea simultaneously. In Palau and other parts of the tropical Pacific, corals of many species tend to synchronize their spawning, usually during the week between the first quarter and the full moon, from April to August. The profusion of eggs, sperm, and larvae of so many species may be a strategy to satiate predators by sacrificing a few, leaving them too full to eat the majority. In parts of Australia's Great Barrier Reef, about 140 species of corals are known to be synchronous, but farther from the equator the synchrony breaks down. In Palau, there is a massive synchronous spawning in April, with smaller pulses every lunar cycle until August. I am watching one of these after-events tonight. This afternoon the polyps of the green brain corals were swollen with imminent brown eggs, and tonight the sea is nearly opaque with the newly erupted ova, which look like yellow and pink berries hanging together on filaments of mucus; I am swimming through the reef's orgy.

A flotilla of comb jellies is also drifting through the swarm, snagging the eggs on clear tenatacles and reeling them into their mouths. The cilia of each comb jelly are coordinated by a few loosely woven neurons to refract the moonlight opalescently, in a series of scintillations that confuse or alarm predators. The jellyfish, therefore, knows the trajectory of sunlight bounced off the maria of the moon and bent by the undulating sea surface as well as the refractive index of the salt sea. It knows the physics of its enemy's eye.

The Palauans, having foraged in this sea for two millennia, also adapt to the Dianic cycle. They know precisely when and where the groupers and other edible species will spawn, and they paddle their outrigger canoes to the reef face to harvest the bounty. To use the poetic metaphor of R. E. Johannes, who in 1977 published *Words of the Lagoon*, a classic treatise on the traditional fishery of Palau, the Palauans understood the ocean's language. The fishermen could identify the species of schooling fish by watching the dipping and diving behavior of the seabirds above. They could perceive the exact, almost imperceptible, moment of slack tide by the orientation of the turquoise damselfish. They took advantage of fish psychology, using kraals woven of palm leaves to herd their quarry into their nets. For open-water fish, these barriers were as terrifying as the barracuda-haunted sea-grass beds. Most important, the Palauan fishermen understood the carrying capacity of the lagoon and devised elaborate oral traditions and prohibitions, known as *bul*, to prevent overfishing. The *bul* were inter-generational works of natural history, crafted according to the rules of reef and tide and designed to protect the fish when they were most vulnerable. Like the storyboards, they were heritage.

Things changed ominously in 1898, when Palau, which had long been a colony of Spain, was purchased by Germany. The German traders introduced goggles to Koror Lagoon, which permitted fishermen to kill more fish with spears. The largest fish in the lagoon began to decline, and the survivors learned to flee at sight of a diver. In the parlance of scuba divers, the Lagoon became "scared." When the Japanese took over Palau in 1914, they introduced other innovations — underwater flashlights, mechanical spear guns, and stationary woven barrier nets. They also made Palau the headquarters of their Pacific colonies. By the 1940s, 50,000 hungry Japanese administrators and military personnel were occupying the islands — five times the indigenous population. Once artisanal and subsistence, the local fishing economy became industrial, and the Palauans became accustomed to the heady world of commerce. Insidious short-term fishing techniques, such as dynamiting and bleach-fishing, were tolerated. The *bul*, and all the knowledge that they represented, were forgotten.

After a series of bloody battles, Palau was relinquished to the United States during the Second World War. The United States administered it as a trust territory until the island nation became independent in 1994. The population of the islands gradually reverted to normal levels, but Koror Lagoon had already been severely strained. The Palauans' culture had also deteriorated. By the time of independence, fully 20 percent of the population was living abroad, mostly in Honolulu and Los Angeles. At the same time, 2,000 foreign workers, most in the service industry, had moved to the islands. The lagoon was yielding a new kind of wealth: tourism, mainly from Japan. Following the patterns of development of Guam and Saipan, there are now plans to build massive resort complexes and to construct an airport able to accommodate 747s flying nonstop from Tokyo.

To some extent, tourism has taken pressure off Koror Lagoon. Reefs with fish accustomed to camera-toting divers are no longer "scared." In the end, tourism could yield far more wealth than the traditional fishing. But without regulation, diving can be as destructive as dynamite. A single anchor, dropped carelessly, can destroy a colony of coral that is a thousand years old. A casual flick of a flipper can cut the protective mucus coating of a coral, making it susceptible to black line disease. The task is to craft modern-day *bul* in the context of contemporary commerce.

*

A forested rock island, hunched like a hedgehog.

174

Peleliu Island is thirty miles south of Babeldoab, still within the protective fringes of Koror Lagoon. In 1944 one of the most savage Pacific battles of the Second World War was fought on its shores. Waves of American Marines stormed the island that June in an effort to dislodge the Japanese from the caves just behind the first dune. The battle, expected to take four days, instead lasted two and a half months. Thirteen thousand boys — Japanese and American — died.

Amber Beach, near Bloody Nose Ridge, Peleliu.

A silent Japanese gun, Peleliu.

At the northern tip of the island is a tranquil village, also named Peleliu, surrounded by plots of taro, their broad leaves shiny in the noonday sun. A gravel road leads south across the forested and uninhabited interior. The roadside is littered with the scraps of war: broken metal helmets, artillery shells, shrapnel. An antiaircraft gun, its barrel rusted to the chassis, lies crumpled in a ditch. The forest is strangely and disconcertingly uniform. The American aerial bombardment and the Japanese artillery leveled the vegetation of Peleliu in 1944. Not a trunk was left standing, and it all regenerated simultaneously in one cohort. Today, the adult trees are all the same age: forty-nine. There are no forest giants here, no old-timers. Not for another half century, if ever, will accident and chance create the treefalls that will restore the full spectrum of light and shadow and therefore the full diversity of Babeldoab's forests.

There is an inshore eddy off eastern Peleliu, beyond the islet of Ngurungor, where the reef fish congregate to release their eggs. It is a place of relative safety. The currents here never carry the offspring very far from shore; after a spin in the plankton, it returns them to their natal reef. During the Marine invasion of Peleliu in 1944, this eddy turned crimson from the blood of American youths cut down by the Japanese soldiers entrenched behind the beach. Those who survived the storming named it "Bloody Beach." A rusted landing craft and a few tanks litter the beach and ridge today. Some of the Japanese never surrendered, and the Marines cemented shut the mouths of their caves, entombing them alive. The caves have never been opened. Other soldiers went feral and lived off the land for years after the American victory. The last Japanese soldier staggered into a taro field outside of Peleliu town in 1964, scaring the daylights out of the women digging the roots. That same day he was tracked down, manacled, and paraded through the village.

I journey to Bloody Beach with five Japanese veterans of that war who have come to pray to their lost comrades. They are mute and seem deeply saddened. What do they think about the tranquility of today? Do they remember the soldiers' awful, youthful passion? A particularly worn old man, bound to a wheelchair and attended by his thirty-year-old grandson, watches rheumily as the sun sequins the eastern sea.

*

The treadless wheels of an abandoned Japanese tank, Peleliu.

The land disappears into them
Covered by the darkness of night
Still it is night.

The Ngmelis Wall is the southern edge of Koror Lagoon, a few miles north of Peleliu, where the abyss reaches up to the shallows. According to the braggadocian fraternity of scuba divers, it is one of the most spectacular dives on earth. On my last day in Palau, I dive solo on the wall. I want to be alone in the wilderness, for a few minutes out of reach of the others of my species. It's a little risky. A solo dive violates every tenet of scuba safety.

The wall is the usual enchanting transition from shallow to deep, lagoon to abyss. I float over its edge into the void, as free as a condor sliding into a thermal. A sand slide, like a white mineral waterfall, tumbles over the rim. The corals below have necrotic patches made by the cascading sand. In the cerulean deep sea, a school of metallic blue jacks courses like a troop of Chinese banner dancers, their lateral lines tasting the little eddies of those in front of them. Two manta rays, turning like dervishes, push their open mouths against the incoming tide, laden with the minuscule animals and plants of the sea pastures. Deeper still, at sixty feet, the cliff face is eroded by caves, where during the day the big-eyed nocturnal fish hide — soldier, cardinal, and squirrel, as red as dusk. Sea fans reach into the dark tide. Their surfaces, unlike those of their shallow-water brethren, are horizontal, so they cross the path of the planktonic layer that rises to the dark surface of the sea each evening and returns at dawn. A few of the fans have folded crinoids clinging to them, dormant, like bunches of string.

At ninety feet I can descend no farther into the wilderness below. There is a profound difference between wilderness and wildness. Wildness can be found everywhere, even in a house fly. Wilderness, by contrast, is complex and sometimes dangerous. Wilderness can consume you. Can the Palauan wilderness survive development, management plans, the compromise of "sustainable" use and economic imperative? Can Palau survive the jet-set tourists? Most of it probably cannot. But wilderness, in little motes here and there, can survive.

It is only 12,000 feet from the top of Antisana in the Andes to the bottom of the Ngmelis Wall, but this small distance encompasses most of the biosphere and the majority of earth's species. This thin film of life, embedded in vapor and liquid, is the only vital zone that we know of in the universe. In many ways, the Ngmelis Wall is a metaphor for the last great places: where a person, one of six billion, can step alone into the wilderness for a little while and, perhaps, become briefly transparent to the affairs of humans, where one can understand the cold indifference of this lovely planet to our lives.

The isolated lakes of the Rock Islands against the long expanse of Koror Lagoon.

References

Moloka'i: The Green Heights of Paliuli

Beckwith, M. W., ed. and trans. 1972. *The Kumulipo, a Hawaiian Creation Chant.* Honolulu: University Press of Hawaii.

Culliney, John L. 1988. *Islands in a Far Sea, Man and Nature in Hawaii.* San Francisco: Sierra Club Books.

Daws, Gavin. 1988. *Hawaii, the Islands of Life.* Honolulu: The Nature Conservancy of Hawaii.

Frame, D., W. L. Wagner, D. R. Herbst, and S. H. Sohmer. 1989. "Hawaiian Islands." In D. G. Campbell and H. D. Hammond, eds., *Floristic Inventory of Tropical Countries,* pp. 181–86. New York: New York Botanical Garden.

"Hog Wild in Hawaii." 1994. *Audubon,* Jan.–Feb., p. 17.

Howarth, F. G., and W. P. Mull. 1992. *Hawaiian Insects and Their Kin.* Honolulu: University of Hawaii Press.

Imada, Clyde T., Warren L. Wagner, and Derral R. Herbst. 1989. "Checklist of Native and Naturalized Flowering Plants of Hawaii." *Bishop Museum Occasional Papers* 29: 31–87.

Meyer, C. S. 1982. *Meyer and Molokai.* Alden, Iowa: Graphic-Agri Business.

Nature Conservancy. 1991. *Pelekunu Preserve Resource Information.* Honolulu: The Nature Conservancy of Hawaii.

Ne, Harriet, with G. L. Cronin. 1992. *Tales of Molokai: The Voice of Harriet Ne.* La'ie, Hawaii: Institute for Polynesian Studies.

Olson, Storrs L., and Helen F. James. 1982. "Fossil Birds from the Hawaiian Islands: Evidence for Wholesale Extinction by Man before Western Contact." *Science* 217: 633–35.

Parks, Noreen. 1993. "The Best Defense Is Da Fence." *Pacific Discovery* 46(3): 12–21.

Price, A. Grenfell, ed. Undated. *The Explorations of Captain James Cook in the Pacific as Told by Selections of His Own Journals, 1768–1799,* pp. 215–25. New York: Heritage Press.

Sohmer, S. H., and R. Gustafson. 1987. *Plants and Flowers of Hawai'i.* Honolulu: University of Hawaii Press.

Stannard, David E. 1989. *Before the Horror: The Population of Hawai'i on the Eve of the Western Contact.* Honolulu: Social Science Research Institute, University of Hawaii.

Cayambe Coca: The Plain of Sky

Brown, Michelle Helyn. 1993. "An Exploratory Study of the Socioeconomic Aspects to Reserve Designation for Volcán Antisana, Ecuador." Master of Science thesis, University of Arizona.

Crosby, Alfred. 1972. *The Columbian Exchange.* Westport, Conn.: Greenwood Press.

Fundación Natura. 1992. *La Reserva Ecologica Cayambe-Coca.* Quito: Fundación Natura.

López R., Susana, coordinator. 1992. *Diagnóstico Socioeconómico de la Reserva Ecológica Cayambe/Coca.* Estudios en Areas Protegidas 2. Quito: Fundación Natura.

Nature Conservancy. Undated. *Ecuador: Sustainable Uses of Biological Resources.* Arlington, Va.: The Nature Conservancy.

Mbaracayú: A Relict in Time

Fundación Moisés Bertoni. 1989. *Analisis Socioeconomico y Cultural de las Poblaciones Asentadas en el Area de Influencia del Proyecto Mbaracayú.* Informe I. Asunción: Fundación Moisés Bertoni.

——. 1992. *Reserva Natural del Bosque Mbaracayú; Plan Operativo 1993–1995.* Asunción: Fundación Moisés Bertoni.

——. 1994. *Proyecto Trinacional de Manejo del Bosque Atlantico Interior. la Etapa. Diagnostico de los Recursos Socio-Ambientales.* Asuncíon: Fundación Moisés Bertoni.

Clastres, Pierre. 1981. *Chronicle of the Guayaki Indians.* New York: Urizen Books.

Hill, Kim R. 1983. "Adult Male Subsistence Strategies among Aché Hunter-Gatherers of Eastern Paraguay." Ph.D. dissertation, University of Utah.

Hill, Kim, and Kristen Hawkes. 1983. "Neotropical Hunting among the Aché of Eastern Paraguay." In R. B. Hames and W. T. Vickers, eds. *Adaptive Responses of Native Amazonians,* pp. 139–88. New York: Academic Press.

Keel, Shirley, Alwyn H. Gentry, and Lucio Spinzi. 1993. "Using Vegetation Analysis to Facilitate the Selection of Conservation Sites in Eastern Paraguay." *Conservation Biology* 7(I): 66–75.

Padwe, Jonathan. 1994. "Mbaracayú — Forest with a Future." *World Birdwatch* 16(2): 16–18.

Guaraqueçaba: Island of the Ice Age

Fonseca, Gustavo A. B. 1985. "The Vanishing Brazilian Atlantic Forest." *Biological Conservation* 34: 17–34.

Mori, Scott A. 1989. "Eastern, Extra-Amazonian Brazil." In David G. Campbell and H. David Hammond, eds. *Floristic Inventory of Tropical Countries,* pp. 181–86. New York: New York Botanical Garden.

Sociedade de Pesquisa em Vida Selvagem. Undated. *Main Features of the Southern Region of Brazil.* Curitiba, Brazil: Sociedade de Pesquisa em Vida Selvagem.

——. 1992. *Plano Integrado de Conservação para a Região de Guaraqueçaba, Paraná, Brasil.* Vols. I and II. Curitiba, Brazil: Sociedade de Pesquisa em Vida Selvagem.

——. 1993. *Guaraqueçaba Atlantic Forest Bioreserve, Brazil. Strategic Plan.* Curitiba, Brazil: Sociedade de Pesquisa em Vida Selvagem and the Nature Conservancy.

The Maya Mountains: The Human Signature

Belize Zoo and Tropical Education Center. 1995. *The Evolution of the Natural Environment of Belize.* Belize City: Belize Zoo.

Hartshorn, G. 1984. *Belize: Country Environmental Profile.* Belize City: Robert Nicolait and Associates.

Partier, T. A., III, B. Holst, L. H. Emmans, and J. R. Meyer. 1993. *A Biological Assessment of the Columbia River Forest Reserve, Toledo District, Belize.* Washington, D.C.: Conservation International.

Río Lagartos: The Ragged Edge of the Continent

Allen, Robert Porter. 1956. *The Flamingoes: Their Life History and Survival.* Research Paper No. 5, National Audubon Society. Hanover, N.H.: Dartmouth Printing Company.

Amigos de la Naturaleza. Undated. *Bioreserve Plan for the Northern and Western Wetlands of the Yucatan Peninsula.* Mérida, Yucatán: Amigos de la Naturaleza.

Stafford, Kathryn. 1994. "Yucatan's Ancient Roots." *Américas* 46(4): 38–43.

The Everglades: Sea of Grass

Boesch, Donald B., Neal E. Armstrong, Christopher F. D'Ella, Nancy G. Maynard, Hans W. Pearl, and Susan L. Williams. 1993. *Deterioration of the Florida Bay Ecosystem: An Evaluation of the Scientific Evidence.* National Fish and Wildlife Foundation, National Park Service, South Florida Water Management District.

Crosby, Alfred. 1972. *The Columbian Exchange.* Westport, Conn.: Greenwood Press.

Davis, Steven M., and John C. Ogden. 1994. *Everglades: The Ecosystem and Its Restoration.* Delray Beach, Fla.: St. Lucie Press.

Durako, Michael J. 1994. "Seagrass Die-off in Florida Bay (USA): Changes in Shoot Demographic Characteristics and Population Dynamics in *Thalassia testudinum.*" *Marine Ecology Progress Series* 110: 59–66.

"Florida Bets on a Boom in Sugar." 1961. *Business Week.* Oct. 14: 58–61.

Florida Department of Natural Resources. Undated. *Fact Sheet. Lignumvitae Key State Botanical Site.* Florida Department of Natural Resources, Division of Recreation and Parks, District 9.

Little, Charles E. 1988. "Rural Clean Water: The Okeechobee Story." *Journal of Soil and Water Conservation* 43: 386–390.

Myers, Ronald L., and John J. Ewel, eds. 1990. *Ecosystems of Florida.* Orlando: University of Central Florida Press.

Nature Conservancy. 1994. *The South Florida Ecosystem Strategic Plan.* Arlington, Va.: The Nature Conservancy.

Robbins, Bradley D., and Susan S. Bell. 1994. "Seagrass Landscapes: Terrestrial Approach to the Marine Subtidal Environment." *Trends in Ecology and Evolution* 9(8): 301–4.

Zieman, J. C. 1982. *The Ecology of the Seagrasses of South Florida: A Community Profile.* Washington, D.C.: U.S. Fish and Wildlife Service, Office of Biological Services.

The Flying D Ranch: Resurrection

Berger, Joel, and Carol Cunningham. 1994. *Bison: Mating and Conservation in Small Populations.* New York: Columbia University Press.

Hornaday, William F. 1889. "The Extermination of the American Bison with a Sketch of Its Discovery and Life History." *Index to the Miscellaneous Documents of the House of Representatives for the First Session of the Fiftieth Congress, 1887–1888.* Washington, D.C.: U.S. Government Printing Office.

The Río San Pedro: The Difference That Water Makes

Crowley, K., and M. Link. 1989. *The Sky Islands of Southeast Arizona.* Stillwater, Minn.: Voyageur Press.

Lowe, Charles H. 1964. *The Vertebrates of Arizona.* Tucson: University of Arizona Press.

Martin, Paul S. 1963. *The Last 10,000 Years.* Tucson: University of Arizona Press.

Palau: The Edge of the Void

Johannes, R. E. 1981. *Words of the Lagoon.* Berkeley: University of California Press.

——. 1991. *Some Suggested Management Initiatives in Palau's Nearshore Fisheries, and the Relevance of Traditional Management.* Hobart, Australia: CSIRO Division of Fisheries.

Kenyon, J. 1993. *Reproduction in Palauan Corals, 1993.* Report prepared for the Nature Conservancy and the Republic of Palau. Koror, Palau: Marine Resources Division.

Myers, R. F. 1989. *Micronesian Reef Fishes.* Barrigada, Guam: Coral Graphics.

Stolzenburg, W. 1994. "The Old Men and the Sea." *Nature Conservancy* 44(6): 16–23.

I am most grateful to Amy Longsworth and Connie Gelb of The Nature Conservancy for their time and effort in helping me on this project. Thanks to Connie Gelb especially for putting me in contact with photographers who had worked closely with The Nature Conservancy in areas where photos were difficult to obtain from other sources.   David Larkin

·

PHOTO CREDITS

American Museum of Natural History, 15

Frederick D. Atwood, 36

E. and P. Bauer (Bruce Coleman, Inc.), 75

Gary Braasch, 81

David G. Campbell, 34–35, 37, 38–39, 46, 55, 57, 61, 72–73, 84, 98–99, 100–1, 106, 114, 118, 126–27, 128, 132–33, 140–41, 175, 176, 177

Bruce Coleman, Inc., 11

Guido Cozzi (Bruce Coleman, Inc.), 22–23, 88, 90

A. J. Dignan (Bruce Coleman, Inc.), 138 top

John S. Flannery (Bruce Coleman, Inc.), 129

Michael Freeman, 9, 26, 70, 93, 96, 97, 102–3, 105, 135, 138 bottom, 142

Peter French (Bruce Coleman, Inc.), 174

Michael Giannechini, 62, 64, 65

Arthur M. Greene (Bruce Coleman, Inc.), 137

Keith Gunnar (Bruce Coleman, Inc.), 17

Stephen Homer, 50 bottom, 52

Dale Knuepfer (Bruce Coleman, Inc.), 78–79

David Larkin, 3

Index